What to Do with
Everything You Own
to Leave the
Legacy You Want

Also by Marni Jameson

Downsizing the Family Home

Downsizing the Family Home: A Workbook

Downsizing the Blended Home

The House Always Wins

House of Havoc

What to Do with

EVERYTHING YOU OWN

—— to Leave the ——

LEGACY YOU WANT

From-the-Heart Estate Planning for Everyone,
Whatever Your Financial Situation

MARNI JAMESON

THE EXPERIMENT

NEW YORK

WHAT TO DO WITH EVERYTHING YOU OWN TO LEAVE THE LEGACY YOU WANT: *From-the-Heart Estate Planning for Everyone, Whatever Your Financial Situation*
Copyright © 2021 by Marni Jameson

The Experiment, LLC, 220 East 23rd Street, Suite 600, New York, NY 10010-4658
theexperimentpublishing.com

This book contains the opinions and ideas of its author. It is intended to provide helpful and informative material on the subjects addressed in the book. *It is not intended to be construed as legal advice. Before making any significant decisions regarding your estate planning, consider seeking the advice of a tax accountant, financial planner, or licensed attorney who specializes in estate law.* This book is sold with the understanding that the author and publisher are not engaged in rendering personal professional services in the book. The author and publisher specifically disclaim all responsibility for any liability, loss, or risk—personal or otherwise—that is incurred as a consequence, directly or indirectly, of the use and application of any of the contents of this book.

The Experiment's books are available at special discounts when purchased in bulk for premiums and sales promotions as well as for fund-raising or educational use. For details, contact us at info@theexperimentpublishing.com.

Library of Congress Cataloging-in-Publication Data

Names: Jameson, Marni, author.
Title: What to do with everything you own to leave the legacy you want : from-the-heart planning for everyone, whatever your financial situation
  Marni Jameson.
Description: New York, NY : The Experiment, LLC, [2021] | Includes index.
Identifiers: LCCN 2021011158 (print) | LCCN 2021011159 (ebook) | ISBN
  9781615197866 (paperback) | ISBN 9781615197873 (ebook)
Subjects: LCSH: Estate planning--United States. | Wills--United States.
Classification: LCC KF750 .J36 2021 (print) | LCC KF750 (ebook) | DDC
  332.024/0160973--dc23
LC record available at https://lccn.loc.gov/2021011158
LC ebook record available at https://lccn.loc.gov/2021011159

ISBN 978-1-61519-786-6
Ebook ISBN 978-1-61519-787-3

Cover design by Beth Bugler
Text design by Sarah Schneider
Cover illustration by iStock.com/Elena Istomina
Author photograph by Tom Burton

Manufactured in the United States of America

First printing June 2021
10 9 8 7 6 5 4 3 2 1

For Doug, always

If you're going to live, leave a legacy. Make a mark on the world that can't be erased.

—MAYA ANGELOU, American poet

CONTENTS

PART THREE: PAINT YOUR CANVAS

What to Do with Everything You Own to Leave the Legacy You Want

Dying Is for Other People

What you leave behind is not what is engraved in stone monuments, but what is woven into the lives of others.

—PERICLES, philosopher, 495–429 BCE

When I was a girl, I used to think only one in ten people really died. As I got older, I thought it was maybe four out of ten, but no one in my family would. Later, I realized the number was closer to seven out of ten, but certainly not me. When my parents died, death became, if not 100 percent certain, a very real possibility.

So, although I, and let's assume you, prefer to imagine we're immune to death, let's just pretend for a moment that we are among those who will die, just hypothetically, of course. Let's imagine, just for discussion's sake, that we walk out the door tomorrow and get struck by a meteor. And let's imagine we have not planned for it, because why would we plan for the unimaginable, for an event that isn't going to happen?

And let's also, for the sake of discussion, assume we have people dear to us, maybe a partner or children, perhaps grandchildren, or we hope to have them. We also have passions and interests, maybe relating to theater or sports or animal rescue, and we have institutions that have meant something to us, that have changed our lives, like a school or a church, or maybe we feel attached and indebted to our hometown. If we were to be among those who die, which we're not, we know we would like to leave something so that these loved ones, or these causes, or these places, will remember us.

But because we don't see the need, since meteor strikes and other means of dying are for other people, we have not prepared. We have no listing of our assets. No one knows we have a safe-deposit box, let alone where the key is. We have no **will**.[*] We have not designated anyone to make a decision if we are on life support and can't speak for ourselves. We have no burial plans. And then, the unthinkable happens.

Because it will. Ready or not.

As I began to write this book, after thinking about it for almost a year, the world was in the throes of a pandemic. The novel coronavirus was grimly gripping the globe. Every day, headlines heralded the latest death toll with ominous forecasts of how many more we could expect to succumb, at home and abroad.

And, like almost everyone in North America, I was sheltering in place, wringing my hands like a wet mop. We were told to

---

*Throughout this book I've highlighted words or phrases that may be new to you, but that are commonly used in the world of wills, estates, and financial planning. I boldfaced the terms the first time they appear in the text to indicate that they also appear in the glossary in chapter 4, a section you may find yourself flipping to often. (I know I did.) Having a handle on these terms will help you make sure you're fluent in legacy lingo when you have important conversations with advisers.

avoid humanity as if contact were lethal. A simple trip to the grocery store could prove fatal. It was a life-altering, world-changing time unlike any I had witnessed, and a truly ideal time to think about what to do with, well, everything we own, to put our angst to good use to think about the unthinkable, our untimely death, as if there were any other kind.

I figured that as long as we all had death and dying on our minds, as long as the pandemic hung over our communities like the sword of Damocles, as long as the Grim Reaper lurked around the corner keeping us shuttered in our homes, I might as well do something productive about it.

Of course, Plan A was: Don't die. For sure that was my plan, and probably yours. But just in case, Plan B was: If we're going to die, let's be organized about it. Don't leave a mess. If we really are going to be dead for longer than we're going to be alive, how we cross the finish line and how we're remembered matter. And that, you can control.

So with the pandemic as a backdrop I began thinking, and talking to others, and writing this book, which I open with the straightforward story of my parents, who died as they had lived, in an exemplary fashion, papers in order. Then I segue to my life afterward, which was not so orderly: My twenty-four-year marriage ended in divorce. I remarried a widowed lawyer. We created a blended family that included my two grown daughters and his three adult children, including a stepson, a child from his late wife's first marriage. So we had a double-blended family. Then those children went out and found partners, and they had more children. Soon I needed a spreadsheet.

While I figured the biggest challenge was going to be keeping all the birthdays straight, my new husband saw a different set of clouds on the horizon. At his urging, I reluctantly went with him headlong into the strange labyrinths of the legal world of **estate planning**, with its marital agreements, wills, **trusts**, and powers of attorney. His singular and notable goal was, and still is, to make sure everyone in the new union is legally protected and fairly treated when our respective times come.

That doesn't just happen.

The result is a book that—whether you're single, married, widowed, divorced, remarried, or somewhere in between; whether you're eighteen or eighty-five; whether you have no children, five children, or someone else's children; whether your family is blended, extended, or upended; whether you have little or much—will light the way with illuminating examples of what to do and not do. It will simplify the complex and offer concrete steps so you can leave this world and those you love with a blessing, not a burden.

Moreover, by helping you better understand not just how to think about your legacy, but also your various options, you will avoid a steep learning curve when you do work on your plan with a legal or financial adviser who charges by the hour. Because your meetings will be more efficient, you will save time and therefore money.

Most important, it will help you figure out what matters, and what to do now to leave the legacy you want later. Because it's not just what you leave, but how you leave it, that matters.

The Golden Age of Giving

This book is also timely because we are in what those in fundraising call the Golden Age of Giving. During the decade between 2017 and 2027, the greatest transfer of wealth in history will occur. Just in the United States, nearly $9 trillion will pass from one generation to the next, according to the *Chronicle of Philanthropy*'s 2018 report.

Here are some more record-breaking statistics:

- As of 2019, American households held about $107 trillion in wealth, up from 2008, during the Great Recession, when household wealth fell to $64.2 trillion (adjusted for inflation).

- More than half of today's wealth, 57 percent, is in the hands of Baby Boomers, those born between 1946 and 1964. This generation amassed significant financial wealth and control roughly 70 percent of all disposable income, according to a 2015 report by *U.S. News & World Report*.*

- Over the next few decades, Baby Boomers will transfer $30 trillion in wealth to younger generations, leading financial experts to refer to the long-term event as the "great wealth transfer." Never before in the history of America, according to *Forbes* magazine, has such a vast amount of wealth moved through the hands of generations.

---

*usnews.com/pubfiles/USNews_Market_Insights_Boomers2015.pdf

Beyond the act of creating a will, or possibly a trust, one of the other themes of this book is to encourage you to consider leaving something, even just 5 percent of your **estate**, to charity. If just 5 percent of that nearly $9 trillion changing hands this decade went to philanthropy, society would benefit from $441 billion going to charitable causes. That's equal to more than eight Bill and Melinda Gates Foundations.

If everyone left just 5 percent to a cause, imagine the impact. But that will only happen if people think about what they care about and what impact they want to have. Now. And for eternity. That's what this book is all about.

Part One

LIVE LIFE ON PURPOSE

The great use of a life is to spend it for something that outlasts it.

—**WILLIAM JAMES**, American philosopher and psychologist (1842–1910)

What do you want your legacy to be? Only you can answer that question, and you should. Once you do, you then need to make it happen. If you don't plan for how you will leave this world, who will? It's not just what you leave, but—probably more important—how you leave it that matters. Read on and begin to take control of your destiny.

CHAPTER 1

Straight Talk About the Facts of Life

How to talk to those you love about death

I n my parents' house the middle drawer of the dresser in the back bedroom contained information about the inconceivable. When my mother first told me about this drawer and its contents, I remember thinking how oddly matter-of-fact she seemed discussing an event so unimaginable and sad. Yet here she was talking about plans she and Dad had made for their dying day as if she were passing along just another perfunctory domestic detail, like her secret gravy recipe or her technique for laundering sheets.

I was in my mid-twenties and some years earlier had moved out of the very bedroom in which I was now standing with my mother, by this middle drawer. I recall trying, probably with only marginal success, to calibrate my expression and voice so my incredulity didn't show through. As I worked to match her matter-of-factness and listen to what she was saying, the same thought kept intruding: "I can't believe we're having this conversation."

The thought of my parents being anywhere but there, together, under that roof, where they'd always been, was, to my mind, simply not an option. They were as permanent and ever present as air.

My older brother and only sibling, Craig, already knew about the drawer and its contents, and Mom said she wanted me to know, too.

Inside the drawer was a neat, fat navy blue plastic envelope with a string closure and the name of a law firm embossed on it in gold letters. Mom took out the package and opened the string tie. Inside were my parents' wills, their life insurance policies, and information about their burial plots.

Then more thoughts joined the *I can't believe we're having this conversation* thought to create a kind of confused chorus: *You already met with an attorney about all this, and I didn't even know?* (Like they were supposed to ask my permission.) *I thought wills were for families of wealth, and our squarely middle-class family isn't one of those.* And finally, *You've already bought your burial plots?* This last thought I blurted out.

"Well, we're going to need them, and we figured it was better we get them than put you and Craig to the trouble."

She had a point, I suppose, but relief wasn't my primary feeling. Unsettled was. Then she pulled out two more envelopes containing policies, one for Craig and one for me. She and Dad had $10,000 life-insurance policies on each of us.

"In case something happens to you kids," she said, again as if discussing the pruning of the rose garden.

"You mean in case *we* die?" I'm sorry, this notion was even further from my mind than having my parents die.

"We want to have enough money to bury you."

I supposed that would come in handy, and I certainly wouldn't want to be a burden. But, sheesh, the whole conversation seemed like much too much adulting, like talk of colonoscopies and cataracts, more topics and eventualities I would just as soon avoid.

Years, later, I looked back at that important conversation as being striking not only for what was said but for how it was said.

As uncomfortable as I was talking about death, especially my parents', my mother's marked nonchalance put death in its place for me. In that moment, I inherited her perspective: Death is something you plan for like you plan for college, or buying a house, or starting a family, or retirement. Her take-it-head-on attitude became my model, and for that legacy I am thankful.

While the discussion could have entailed a fair amount of hedging and hemming, or the awkwardness of a parent explaining the facts of life to a child (and what is death but a fact of life?), my mom, a former army nurse, delivered the news with unvarnished pragmatism.

That became my attitude, too. That day my mother's unspoken message spoke loudly, and left this legacy: This is how our family does death. And this is how you talk to the people whom you will leave about what you will leave when you do leave.

Of course, that unimaginable day did come, but not for thirty years after that conversation in the bedroom. Dad died in 2013 at age ninety, and Mom in 2016 at age ninety-four. Thanks

Death is something you plan for, like you plan for college, or buying a house, or starting a family, or retirement.

to their practical foresight, my brother and I knew what to do. Although losing them wasn't easy, they had made it a lot easier.

And so can we.

In my family, the assets were modest, and the will straightforward. All assets were to be equally divided between my brother and me, and to stay in our bloodline. Craig, being the oldest, was named the **executor**, the one appointed to carry out the terms of the will.

He had taken over the handling of our parents' financial affairs as they moved into assisted living. Fortunately, Dad was still able to talk him through much of it as he handed over the reins. I took on the task of clearing out and selling the family home to help finance their long-term care.

While not easy, all went according to my parents' well-made plans. But that's not always the case. As you'll see in the chapters ahead, even with the best of plans, the wishes of the departed don't always play out so smoothly. Lack of paperwork, incomplete paperwork, conflicting paperwork, lack of cooperation, miscommunication, greedy relatives, and feuding heirs have led to some of the most expensive legal battles in history, dividing families irreparably and redirecting huge sums of money away from deserving family members or worthy causes and into lawyers' bank accounts.

Although the family I grew up in was traditional in every sense— intact, nuclear, two kids—my own life going forward would be much different and would involve divorce, stepkids, and remarriage, all commonplace but complicating factors that make careful planning and paperwork even more important.

As one estate planning expert I spoke with told me, the difference between dying with your affairs in order and dying without them is like leaving your loved ones with a thousand-piece jigsaw puzzle to put together after you're gone. In the first case, they have a picture of the puzzle they're assembling, but in the second, they don't.

CHAPTER 2

What About Me?

Estate planning for nontraditional families—in other words, most of us

---

Though traditional nuclear families of modest means may be the simplest type of entity to create an estate plan for, they're not the norm. The blended family is. In the United States, the so-called nontraditional family—that is, families with single parents, cohabiting couples, and stepfamilies—now outnumber "traditional" ones, according to Smart Stepfamilies, an organization that studies, educates, and supports stepfamilies, noting that 40 percent of married couples with children have at least one child from a prior relationship. That number increases when you factor in cohabitating couples. These blended families, while common, introduce a whole new set of dynamics, and often form the basis for the dark stuff of fairy tales.

So I learned when I married DC in 2016 and we became a blended-blended family with five grown children ages twenty-one to thirty-four at the time. A widower, DC had a son, a daughter, and a stepson. I was divorced with two daughters.

I first realized the situation could be complicated when we were having dinner one night early in our dating relationship and DC announced he was going to set up a trust to "protect his kids."

I remember sitting across from him trying to summon everything I knew about trusts, which took less than three seconds. In my mind, trusts were something that ultra-wealthy people left for their kids to live off and fight over. Since that was far from my reality, I had never given creating a trust any thought.

I knew that DC was comfortable, but I didn't get the sense that he had vast assets, or that we were greatly misaligned financially. So I asked, "How come?" Secretly, I worried that his kids viewed me as a financial threat, as some interloper bent on squandering the family assets. Or worse, maybe he did? *Should I be offended?* DC explained: "I want to protect them—and you—from doubt."

Turned out that a sincere and legitimate question from Adam, his stepson, had prompted the decision to create a trust, which was a good idea.

Trusts create trust

When DC married his first wife, he was twenty-seven and just out of law school. His wife was twenty-eight and divorced, with a five-year-old. DC became a stepdad to Adam, who lived with his mom and DC during the school year and with his biological father over the summer. Adam called both men Dad, and still does.

Then DC and his wife had two more children, Alyssa and Brett. All three kids grew up together, and the blended bunch were very much a family, except that Adam had two dads. Because Adam's biological father stayed involved in his life, helped support him, and maintained all his paternal rights, DC never adopted Adam.

When DC's wife died of lung cancer in 2013, at age fifty-five, Adam, who was thirty-two then and married with his own young family, wondered where that left him.

"What about me?" he wanted to know. Now that DC held all the marital assets, would Adam be entitled to any inheritance from this family now that his mom was gone, or would he be orphaned and left out? What if DC remarried? Would the new wife get whatever portion should have gone to him, or worse, squander it?

Adam's good question prompted DC to put a vehicle in place to reassure the kids that they were taken care of. A trust, designating his three children as beneficiaries, would eliminate any concern that some other woman was going to swoop down and deprive them of what was theirs.

As DC and I grew more serious, this move eventually led us to talk about organizing our respective and (potentially one day) combined assets into three buckets, which we referred to as "yours, mine, and ours."

I later came to appreciate that by creating a trust for his kids, DC also shielded the new wife—ultimately me—from any suspicion or accusation that she might misappropriate any-thing meant for the kids. (Court cases involving estate and trust matters are sadly rife with stories of women with children who remarry men with children, and when the man dies first, the wife redirects all the funds to her kids, leaving his out. That wasn't going to happen here.)

Though the insinuation was disturbing, I soon saw that it beat the alternative—being suspected of foul play. This could, of course, happen in reverse. If I died first and DC inherited 100 percent of what I had brought to the marriage, he could leave my kids out. You'll see later how we dealt with that.

Although I never think of these selfish scenarios, fortunately others, like DC, are trained to spot trouble and head it off at the gate. Being a lawyer, he has seen the darker sides of humanity, and what greed can do.

So DC went to a trusts and estates lawyer, and had him draw up a revocable **living trust** (you'll read more about trusts in part three), meaning that as long as he's alive he can access the funds or change the terms. The document is tied to his will, which basically says, "See the trust."

While every blended relationship has to create its own fair formula, here's how we did it.

Yours, mine, and ours

We ultimately created three trusts. One for his kids, one for mine, and a joint trust for all.

The trust for DC's adult children earmarks a portion of DC's premarital assets for his children to get when he dies, even if I'm still alive. That trust includes a portion of the proceeds from the sale of the house he and his late wife owned, along with a portion of their joint savings. He manages those funds and invests them to help the fund grow. He occasionally uses the funds to loan his kids money.

Upon DC's death, the assets in the trust will be divided among his three children forty-forty-twenty. Forty percent to each biological child and 20 percent to Adam, who has two fathers to inherit from. As the only biological child of his natural father, Adam is presumably in line to receive an inheritance from him that his half-siblings wouldn't get. That situation is what estate lawyers call a **"bright line,"** and it helps establish fair distribution in blended situations.

With a trust established, DC could reassure his adult children that he had money set aside for them in honor of their mom and their marriage, and that those funds were legally protected. He could also move forward into remarriage with those potential issues resolved.

As we moved closer to marriage, we agreed—well, let's be honest, he advised and I required some convincing—that we needed to hire a lawyer to draw up even more legal documents: a trust for my daughters, another for us, two **advance healthcare directives**, and a premarital agreement.

Welcome to life with a lawyer.

We created a second revocable living trust for my daughters in my name, setting aside a portion of what I inherited from my parents and some other premarital funds for them to receive fifty-fifty when I die. I try to manage that fund, investing in a bit of real estate, so it will grow.

Our remaining nonretirement assets, mainly our house, are held jointly, and we corralled those into a third living trust that will ultimately be divided among all five—22/22/22/22/12. Finally, we both took out term life-insurance policies naming each other as beneficiaries.

What a gift. Everyone is protected and no one can accuse a stepparent of overstepping.

But we still weren't done.

You want me to sign what?!

We signed one more paper, one that couples often find to be more unsettling than writing a will. We signed a **prenuptial agreement**. Once again, I had a lot to learn about the purpose of this notorious document, the stuff of television dramas, and not a little resistance to overcome.

See, I'd always thought prenuptial agreements were for couples who didn't trust each other, who married under a cloud of suspicion, or for those with a tremendous financial imbalance. ("He just married her for her money.") They seemed to get marriages off to an inauspicious start. That's certainly not where I was coming from, and I admit that I felt a little injured by the suggestion. Granted, I was divorced, so knew as well as anyone that the inconceivable could happen, but did that make me dishonorable?

And would signing these papers mean that if DC left me after I'd invested twenty years in our marriage I would be exposed and destitute? The fact that I had lawyers surrounding me didn't diminish my feelings of insecurity. To generate this document, DC and I had to hire separate lawyers, so each of us would be represented. That, too, felt strange, like a divorce rehearsal. Being a lawyer, he was at home in this world, but I felt as if I were trying to communicate underwater in Latin.

However, as we discussed it, I soon saw that this was about protecting the kids, too, as well as being fair. The prenuptial or premarital agreement, as it's sometimes called, allowed us to identify those assets that we were separately bringing to the marriage. These became the "yours" and "mine" buckets that formed the bases for our respective trusts. The agreement was designed to make sure they stayed there.

By design, this agreement would prevent either of us from raiding the other's assets should the unexpected occur. The trickle-down effect would mean added security for our respective children just in case the marriage didn't work out, not that either of us expected that to occur. I needed to swallow this with more than one glass of wine, but ultimately my anxiety lessened and I trusted DC to do right by us all, which he did.

Like so many other myths I broke through during this process, I learned that these agreements weren't just for other people. They can in fact fortify a marriage, and particularly a remarriage where kids are involved.

My parents' situation, which I described, was simple. And in my prior marriage, my husband and I had started out like most young newlyweds—with more debts than assets. We didn't have a prenuptial agreement because we had nothing to protect. We never drew up a will, not even after we had kids, partly because we lived in a **community-property** state and figured that if either of us died, the other would get everything. In the nine states that have community-property law, all assets acquired during the marriage belong to each spouse fifty-fifty. (Still, as you will see, this is not a good reason to not have a will.)

But the driving reason we did not have a will was because my ex rejected the idea. Like so many people, he didn't want to discuss the subject. I was uneasy about that—but didn't press it. Fortunately, we never had to test what happens when you don't have a valid will in place and you die and leave minor children, a circumstance we'll talk more about in the chapters ahead.

Now it was different. Today, DC and I have yours, mine, and ours buckets that feel protected and fair. Everyone in the family knows they are entitled to an appropriate portion of the estate someday, and each child knows how they fit into this crazy quilt tapestry of ours.

They know because, just as my mom did with me, we told them.

CHAPTER 3

When You Are Engulfed in Flames

Getting your papers in order

Prompting my uncharacteristically lucid and rational thoughts on the subject of organized dying was, naturally, that lucid and rational lawyer I live with.

On one of those many days in the long string of days we spent sheltering in place during the pandemic, I came upon him typing diligently on his laptop at the kitchen table, his adopted office. I looked over his shoulder and saw the document title: "In Case of Death."

"Oh, for heaven's sake," I said.

"What?" he said. "You're going to need this someday, and you're going to thank me." DC is a young sixty-two and has decades left, as far as I'm concerned. But having lost his first wife, he knows what can happen.

I scanned the contents, which include what attorney to call in case he's killed in an accident.

"Fine," I said, resigned, "write one for me, too, while you're at it, in case I go first, except title mine: 'When You Are Engulfed in Flames.'"

I borrowed the title from a book by humorist David Sedaris, who, in one of the book's essays, describes finding in a Hiroshima hotel room awkwardly translated literature explaining what to do in case of an emergency. The safety booklet is titled "Best Knowledge of Disaster Damage Prevention and Favors to Ask of You." The in-case-of-fire section has a subhead that reads, "When You Are Engulfed in Flames" and then dryly goes on to explain what to do. This cracks me up every time. It also aptly describes my emergency planning strategy.

The point, of course, is this: Get your exit plan together before you are engulfed in flames, before you get hit by that meteor—in other words, before it's too late, and, ideally, many years before you need it.

So DC makes his folder "In Case of Death," and I have mine, "When You Are Engulfed in Flames," and to elevate them appropriately, I put them in a decorative accordion file, one that has a glossy botanical pattern on it and a pretty latch, and is not banker brown. (When I go, I plan to go in style.)

As we think about what all to include, it strikes me that for all the organizing and downsizing advice I have imparted in almost eighteen years of writing a weekly home-and-lifestyle column, for all the tips I've espoused over the years, whether for closets or kitchens or offices or garages, I have never publicly tackled this most important organizing act of all, the ultimate downsizing, as it were.

While not *easy*, in some respects this downsizing project is *easier* than others. Unlike most downsizing projects, which require physical work—taking boxes to Goodwill, hauling old furniture to the curb—this all-important downsizing task is a relatively light lift. All you need to pick up is a phone, a pen, and some papers.

So I called Amy Davis, a wealth adviser with Resource Consulting Group in Orlando, who is also an attorney, certified public accountant, and Certified Financial Planner, and asked her what all we should pull together so our loved ones have a road map, and why.

Davis is the one who provided the earlier jigsaw-puzzle analogy and had me imagine pouring out the pieces to a thousand-piece jigsaw puzzle and trying to assemble them without the benefit of a picture. "That's what it's like for loved ones left without a plan."

A will and an estate plan provide the picture, and help your loved ones put the pieces together a lot faster, she said. The section at the end of this chapter lists the pieces she suggests you pull together and put in your meteor box. Davis also encourages those of you looking to meet with an adviser to make the most of that first appointment by having all of your financial documents in hand. You'll find a checklist of what to bring to your first meeting in the appendix at the back of this book.

What matters?

Before diving into the whys and wherefores of an estate plan, first do some reflecting, Davis said. "Ask yourself some philosophical questions, like what are my values, what's important, what am I grateful for?" Look at your life and connections and determine who and what matters.

For most people, the priorities are, first, to take care of themselves and their spouse or partner, next to take care of their kids, and third to support their causes. Then the goal becomes "how to fill those buckets," said Davis.

After outlining what matters, use the worksheets in the appendix to take an inventory of all you have. List every asset, including real estate, savings and checking accounts, investments, retirement accounts—IRAs and 401(k)s—and pensions. Now include any relevant insurance policies, including life insurance and long-term-care coverage.

Then list whom (or what) you would like to acknowledge: living children, including those who are still dependent, and other loved ones, including aging parents and pets you care for, and the causes you want to support.

Once you figure out what you have, and whom you want to benefit (including causes), the next step is to declare those goals and find the most efficient way to realize them. Two worksheets in the appendix will help you get a snapshot of your assets, and also get you thinking about what matters to you. For most people who have children, their kids are the primary beneficiaries, but after they're taken care of, maybe you could consider doing more?

The famous line in estate and tax law is "I want to leave my kids enough to be independent, but not so much they don't have to work." The magic question, of course, then becomes: How much is that? We'll tackle that topic a bit more in chapter 13. Meanwhile, I hope this book gets you thinking about maybe leaving behind a little more for causes that mean something to you. You'll see inspiring examples in this book in which the smallest gestures have turned into meaningful legacies that have gone on for generations.

Prepare for the Meteor

I know, none of us is planning on dying. It's certainly not on my list. But we should, for the sake of our loved ones, plan for a day when we walk out the door and get struck by a meteor. That means having your "stuff" together. Here's what everyone, regardless of age or circumstance, should pull together into one organized place:

- **Contact information for trusted advisers.** (Use the worksheet in the appendix to list yours.) Your loved ones, your executor, or whoever is in charge of your affairs will need access to your legal and financial information, so point that person in the right direction. Put the name and current contact information of your accountant or attorney, and your **personal representative**, if you have one, right on top. (See chapters 6 and 11 for more about naming your executor or personal representative.)

- **Your will.** Everyone should have one. A will simply advises and coordinates the distribution of your assets when you die, so the state doesn't do the job for you. It also names guardians for minor children. (See chapter 11 for a fuller explanation of wills.)

- **Trust documents (if you have them).** A key difference between a will and a trust is that a will is a public document, meaning that one could gain access to a dead person's will by contacting the clerk of courts in the county where the will was filed. Finding it may take a little digging, but the records are often available online. Many of the assets named in a will must also go through **probate** (which we'll also cover more in chapter 12). What you spell out in your will is open to the public. If you don't want the world to know you left Cousin Susie $50,000, set up a trust, then say in your will that all directives are in your trust. (We'll talk more about trusts in chapter 11.)

- **Your prenuptial agreement (if you have one).**

- **A list of assets.** Create an inventory of your bank accounts— savings, checking, retirement—and include where they're held, account numbers, how to access these accounts, and the names of any beneficiaries. Include documentation on other assets, such as real estate, stocks, annuities, pensions, life-insurance policies, and any other pockets where you have resources tucked away. Don't forget to include fine jewelry, artwork, and collectibles, which we'll talk more about in Part Four. Use the "What Do I Have?" and "Asset Inventory" worksheets in the appendix to get started.

- **Safe-deposit box information.** If you have a safe-deposit box, list its contents, include photographs of them, and say who has access to it and where the key is. Absent a court order, the only people authorized to open the safe-deposit box are those whose names are on the account and signature card. As a precaution, see if you can arrange for the box to be accessed if not by just you, by two people together. (See chapter 10 for more on safe-deposit-box safeguards.)

- **Digital access.** Because so much of our important information lies locked within our mobile phones and computers, be sure your trusted person knows where to find your usernames and passwords to get into these online records. Also list all the online subscriptions you have that should be cancelled, like Amazon Prime, Hulu, and companies that automatically charge your credit card or auto-renew memberships, and also all of your active social media accounts. Designate someone to be your surrogate administrator on social media accounts to close them. This can be done informally, by simply asking someone you trust—an assistant or colleague, your partner, a good friend, or one of your children. Because when you die, your privacy may not die with you.

- **An ethical letter.** Sometimes called an ethical will, an **ethical letter** is a letter that supplements your will and explains why you did what you did, Davis said. "It's a 'here's what I was thinking' letter." Although not legally binding, it's an opportunity for you to clarify why you left more or less to one relative or another, or chose one guardian over someone else, or chose to leave assets to a certain cause. "This letter is the last communication your family will have from you, and it's where you can share your thoughts and values." Ideally, nothing in this letter will come as a surprise, as you will have had "the conversation" with your family before this day. (See chapter 13 for more on avoiding surprises.)

- **Household bills.** Use the worksheet in the appendix to make a list of all the bills and people you pay regularly and how, from the electric bill to the lawn service. Also list your outstanding debts, including taxes owed. Your survivors likely won't be obligated to pay debts that benefited only you, like, say, your laser eye surgery. But your partner may be responsible for paying off any debt that benefited you both, like the vacation you took together.

- **Durable power of attorney.** If you want someone to act as your agent, to handle your bills and oversee your affairs when you become incapable of making financial decisions, spell that out in a durable power of attorney. Add this name to other important contacts at the front of the file.

- **Advance directives.** This document, also known as a **living will**, conveys your end-of-life wishes, relieving loved ones of the need to make tough calls about life-support choices because you have already made them. Here you can name whomever you want to be in charge of your end-of-life decisions if you can't be. "It doesn't have to be your closest relative," adviser Amy Davis said. "Sometimes it's better if it is not." (See chapter 4 for more about durable power of attorney and advance directives.)

Put everything together in a safe place, like a strongbox, home safe, safe-deposit box, or even an accordion file. Do not store important papers anywhere that could get damp, humid, or excessively hot, so not in unfinished attics or basements. Then be sure the right people—trusted family members or representatives—know where they are.

What matters?

When creating an estate plan, one of the first steps you need to take is to define your goals. In addition to taking care of your loved ones, for instance, a goal might be to minimize the taxes your estate will owe after you die, thus leaving more money for the people or causes you love. Another goal might be to avoid or minimize probate, a legal process whereby the court serves as a sort of clearinghouse for your assets and is responsible for handling them. Perhaps you want to keep creditors and other interlopers (like estranged ex-family members) from getting undeserved sums. Those are all fine goals, but is there more to be thinking about? When creating your legacy, think beyond the immediate and obvious and ask what else matters to you. Where else could you leave a gift that could make a lasting difference, one that could change lives, advance research, support the arts, heal the environment, help those less fortunate? This takes some soul searching. But if you are going to paint your own canvas and leave a legacy beyond your family, as we'll discuss later, you need to design your plan so you remember critical causes in your will and, conversely, so you are remembered.

I'll admit, when I started this book I did not have a strong feeling about where I might want to leave just 5 percent of my estate. After taking care of my kids, where else could I leave a gift that could make a difference? I had interests, sure, but I didn't have a strong passion, or a sense that I could make a difference anywhere.

I don't expect you to have that answer right away, but the questions in the "Values Worksheet: What Matters?" in the appendix will help you start thinking about where your legacy might lie. To answer the question, "How do I want to be remembered?" think about the people, places, and opportunities that have changed your life. A look at where you spend and have spent your time and money may also reveal what you value.

Take some time in filling out this worksheet. The prompts are designed to get you thinking. This is your legacy, not mine.

CHAPTER 4

Words to Live (and Die) By

The legal lingo

The first time I sat in a room with an attorney discussing trust documents, I felt like I was watching a foreign film, searching for subtitles. Although I'm educated and consider myself reasonably intelligent, I was completely at sea, with nary a float to grab onto, because I lacked the language. As a writer, I know that words are keys that open doors to understanding.

See, probably like you, I came to this subject—the legal aspects of estate planning—not as one who does this for a living, but as someone curious, uninitiated, and motivated to learn. I don't need to know as much as an estate lawyer does, but I do want to know enough to have an intelligent conversation with one.

For that, I—and now you—first had to learn the lingo.

I drew on my reporting skills, asked experts a lot of questions, and leaned, not a little, on my attorney husband's expertise to put together a glossary. The following glossary provides words that I want you to look at as handles. These handles open doors to concepts as well as to conversations. If you can use these words when talking with financial planners, tax advisers, and attorneys, you'll be speaking their language. Knowing these terms helps you literally get on the same page as your advisers. Read this section now, then bookmark it for easy reference as you continue reading. You'll likely want to flip back here as we use these terms again.

After we get the vernacular down, we'll get to the stories of successful and creative ways folks have designed their legacies, and also a few spectacularly unsuccessful attempts, but first, the vocabulary primer.

Words to know before you talk to an expert

This book is not designed to take the place of working with an attorney who specializes in wills, trusts, and estates. However, it will give you a running start and will help you have an intelligent, informed conversation with a professional when you do. Becoming fluent in their language and knowing what basic terms mean can save you from paying an adviser $300 an hour to explain.

While you won't be ready to take the bar exam, you will be able to talk intelligently to legal and financial advisers, which will empower you to understand the pieces in play.

The Glossary

advance health-care directive: Also called an advance directive, this document lets you spell out your wishes for end-of-life decisions before you can't physically or mentally make such decisions yourself. These directives are in effect when you're alive. They help family members, or your **health-care proxy**, make decisions—based on your wishes—about what medical lengths to go to in order to prolong your life. While some want every measure taken, others want to forgo heroic measures to, among other reasons, avoid depleting resources (money spent on end-of-life care) that they would rather leave to their heirs.

beneficiary: A fancy word for the person, charity, or other organization that will inherit an asset. When this person is a family member, he or she is also called an heir.

bright line: A term lawyers use to refer to a set of objective facts that offer a clear demarcation and that allow for little to no question as to their interpretation by the courts.

charitable donor-advised fund: An investment fund created for the sole purpose of supporting charities of your choice. Whatever you contribute (cash, stocks, or securities, for example) to the fund is immediately tax-deductible and can grow tax-free. However, funds are irrevocable; you cannot take the money out for personal use. You can only use them to support an IRS-qualified public charity. According to the investment firm Fidelity, donor-advised funds are the fastest-growing charitable-giving vehicle in the United States because they are one of the easiest and most tax-advantageous ways to give to charity.

charitable gift annuity: A contract between a donor and a charitable organization that guarantees the charity will invest the gift and make annuity payments to the donor or designated beneficiaries for a period of time, usually the lifetime of the donor or the beneficiaries. The amount left at the end of that time stays with charity.

charitable lead trust: An irrevocable trust that provides financial support to one or more charities for a set number of years, after which time what is left of the assets (the remainder) goes to family members or to other non-charity beneficiaries. This may be a good vehicle for heirs who can afford to wait to receive their inheritance.

charitable life estate: For those who want to leave their house to a charity, this arrangement allows the donor to continue living in the home after they donate it.

charitable remainder trust: An irrevocable trust (meaning that you can't take the money back) that is donated to a charity, but that is set up to pay the donor or a named beneficiary an income stream over a period of years, usually no more than twenty. This helps partially reduce taxes. When the donor or the last beneficiary dies, the remainder goes to the charity.

codicil: A change made to a will. This addition keeps the original will in place but adds to or changes it. (A change made to a *trust* is an amendment.)

community property: A state law that considers all assets that a married couple acquires during their marriage community property, meaning that each spouse owns half. States having community property laws are Arizona, California, Idaho, Louisiana, Nevada, New Mexico, Texas, Washington, and Wisconsin.*

---

*By FindLaw Staff, reviewed by Kellie Pantekoek, Esq., last updated May 19, 2020

corpus: The body of assets contained in a trust.

decedent: The term used in legal circles to refer to the person who died—the deceased.

designated fund: An arrangement where a donor gives a financial gift to a foundation, such as a community foundation, or to a corporate fund manager to disburse contributions on a donor's behalf. The fund manager uses the funds to support charities of the donor's choice both while the donor is alive and after they die. Donors get to see the benefits of their gifts in their lifetime.

durable power of attorney: *See* power of attorney.

endowment: A sum of money or other financial asset donated to nonprofit organizations, churches, hospitals, or universities to create an investment fund. The money is invested so that the principle grows and provides future income into perpetuity.

estate: Everything you own.

estate plan: A set of documents wherein you name your beneficiaries and arrange for your assets to be distributed among them. In general, the documents include the will or trust papers, a power of attorney statement, beneficiary designations, an ethical letter, health-care power of attorney declaration, and guardianship designations. Ideally (emphasis on "ideally"), a well-thought-out estate plan helps reduce tax liability, limits what goes through probate (see below), eliminates confusion or arguments among family members, and ensures that the causes that matter to you will benefit according to your wishes.

estate and inheritance tax: A tax many states and the federal government impose on assets passed to beneficiaries after a person's death. Most heirs never pay the federal tax, because if the deceased's estate is worth less than $11.58 million (as of this writing), it falls below the tax threshold. If the estate is over that amount, heirs only pay estate taxes (up to 40 percent) on the amount above $11.58 million. Note, however, that this dollar amount has changed many times over the years as tax laws change, and it could change again, which is another reason to involve a financial adviser when planning your estate. State laws vary, and some have a lower threshold for the amount subject to taxation. (See chapter 12 for a list of states that have estate and inheritance taxes.)

ethical letter: Also called a letter of intent or ethical will, this is a letter left to your heirs that supplements your will and explains what you were thinking when you set up your will as you did. Although usually not legally binding, it may help inform a probate judge of your intentions and may help in the distribution of your assets if the will is in question.

executor: Also called a personal representative depending on the state, an executor is the person designated in the will to carry out its terms, or to "execute" the will. When the author of the will (the testator) dies, the executor takes over paying any outstanding bills and taxes, clears any property liens, and sells property in order to collect and distribute assets. The executor does all of this as part of a legal process called probate. (*See* probate.) The executor picks up where the power of attorney leaves off, and is often the same person. But unlike a power of attorney, an executor does not make decisions for you, but rather only executes the directions that you state in your will.

health-care proxy: This is the person you choose to be legally responsible for making your health-care decisions if you can't. This is often a family member or trusted friend, but not always. To name your health-care proxy, you need to fill out a specific legal document to that effect.

intestate: When a person dies without a will, he or she is said to have died intestate. In this common situation, the court in the state where that person lived will appoint someone to oversee the distribution of the assets according to that state's laws.

le mort main: French for "the dead hand," a term that refers to having influence or control after you're gone.

living trust: Also called a revocable living trust, this form of trust allows the owner (the settlor) to change the terms, access the funds, and manage the assets while he or she is living. Once the owner dies, the trust becomes irrevocable. For tax purposes, some individuals set up an irrevocable trust while they're living, but once they do, they give up access to those assets. (See chapter 11 for a fuller discussion of trusts).

living probate: A legal action permitted in a handful of states, living probate allows residents of those states to have a court review their will while they are alive to determine its validity. This gives authors of a will a chance to make clarifications while they are alive, and it reduces the chances of a challenge to the will later.

non-probate will substitute: These are assets that are not included in a will or a trust and that also don't go through probate. They are probate-dodging vehicles that offer a free pass. What these assets typically have in common is a named beneficiary. Common examples include retirement accounts, bank accounts, and life insurance.

personal representative: *See* executor.

planned gift: A donation commonly designated in a will or trust to go to a specific charity or cause at a future time, usually right after the donor dies.

power of attorney/durable power of attorney: This document gives another person the power to make legal decisions on your behalf and to act as your agent when you can't. This power can be limited to one type of decision, say the sale of a property, or it can be broader. The power of attorney takes effect once you can no longer make decisions. Unless revoked, it extends this person's rights up until your death. You must name this person, however, when you are in a sound state of mind. Once you die, your executor has power of attorney over your assets based on the duties and powers spelled out in the will.

power of variance: If a charity or other donor-designated cause changes its direction or mission after you die and that new direction is no longer aligned with your wishes, or if the organization closes, the power of variance rule allows those handling your funds to adapt and redirect funds to another cause in line with your intentions.

prenuptial agreement: A legal agreement between a couple engaged to be married that determines how marital, particularly premarital, assets will be divided in the case of a divorce. A postnuptial agreement is for couples who want to revise a prenuptial agreement or create a similar legal agreement after they're married or have entered into a civil union.

probate: When a person dies, whether he or she has a will or not, certain assets will need to go through probate, a legal process the court oversees that serves as a clearinghouse for that person's belongings. The point of probate is to make sure all the person's debts are settled and financial obligations are met before assets get distributed to heirs. The process involves validating the will, locating the executor and beneficiaries, finding and evaluating all assets, paying debts and taxes the person who died owes, then distributing the remaining assets to the beneficiaries. The process can be time-consuming and costly. Probate is also a public process, which means personal financial matters may no longer be private. As a result, many legal experts work to help their clients and their beneficiaries avoid probate by creating a trust.

quitclaim: This is a legal document that officially ends ownership of a piece of real estate so ownership can transfer. This allows owners to give up their claim to a piece of property. For example, if you own a house and want that property to be in the trust, you need to file a quitclaim, so the trust can become the owner. Married couples who own a home together and later divorce also use quitclaim deeds when one party is going to have sole ownership of the house.

settlor (or owner): The person who creates and funds the trust (usually with the help of an attorney) and who owns the assets in the trust.

testator: The owner or author of a will, the person bequeathing his or her wishes and signing the will.

title: How a property is legally owned. Typical ways of taking title include joint tenants with rights of survivorship, tenancy by the entireties, tenants in common, community property, and sole ownership. (See chapter 14 for more about titles.)

trust: A legal entity that holds assets on behalf of a settlor who uses the trust to dispense assets to named beneficiaries, such as children or charities. Trusts can dictate when and how assets get disbursed. Unlike wills, which are public records, trusts are for the most part private. (The exception is a testamentary trust, which is created by a will and is subject to probate, and thus not private.) If you don't want the world to know how much you left to whom, set up a trust. Assets that flow through trusts typically bypass probate, saving time, court fees, and sometimes estate taxes. The two main types of trust are revocable and irrevocable. (See chapter 11 for more on trusts).

trustee: The person the settlor names to administer the trust, and to make distributions to the beneficiaries as expressed in the trust.

will: A legal document that advises how you (or a testator) would like your assets divided when you die. A will names an executor, or personal representative, to carry out the will's provisions, names beneficiaries, includes instructions for how to disburse assets, and appoints a guardian when minor children are left.

Phew! Now that *that's* over with, on to some stories about people, their stuff, their dreams, and their legacies. But do refer to this glossary as we move forward.

Part Two

HOW THEY
DID IT

An object in motion stays in motion.

—ISAAC NEWTON, English mathematician and physicist
(1643–1727)

Scenarios vary widely, from those who have just a little to those who have much, from single folks with no children to triple-blended families with kids, grandkids, and great-grandkids. The chapters ahead feature true stories of the diverse and creative ways individuals from different walks have created their legacies.

CHAPTER 5

Free to a Good Home

Even if you don't have a Picasso,
you can still help your museum

A museum executive called me shortly after my book *Downsizing the Family Home* came out to ask if I would give the keynote talk at a community event she was planning, I thought, *Why me?*

"You want me to talk about downsizing?" I asked, making sure the caller, Emily Blaugrund Fox, executive director of Albuquerque Museum Foundation, had the right person.

"Yes, clearing out the family home," she verified.

That was my expertise all right, but I was puzzled. I was thinking downsizing as in clearing out all the stuff that accumulates in a family home over decades—books you'll never read again or at all, old televisions with lost remotes, faded, frayed towels, so-so artwork, passé clothes, baby toys belonging to the kid who now drives, assorted vases so plentiful you could open a flower shop, toothless rakes—the stuff of life we're so good at acquiring and not so good at letting go of.

"If they have items of value, we'd like them to think of the museum when they do their estate planning," Fox said. She later told me that another option would be to arrange to have all their belongings liquidated after they die and then have the proceeds go to the museum, and shortly we'll meet a couple who plans to do just that.

"Ooohhhh, right! Stuff of *value*." I wasn't making the connection because we don't have stuff of value in my family. Like most households, we just have stuff of no value. I do, however, have family members who *think* some of their stuff has value, but it wouldn't fetch two fly wings at a flea market; just don't tell them that.

"If they have valuable pieces of art, or a historic artifact from the region that they think would be a fit for our mission, we'd like them to call us," she said.

"Do people often think they have something precious that isn't?" I asked, but I'm thinking, *Like everyone*.

"Our curators will be honest," she said. "While we don't want grandma's cross-stitched hankies, if you have an old piece of Indian pottery from the area, we might take a look."

All this got me thinking, *What could I tell these museum types about how to bequeath beloved belongings?*

For more perspective, I called Graydon Sikes, a fine-art appraiser in Cincinnati, and co-owner of Caza Sikes.

"While most households don't have anything of significant value, when we review an estate, we sometimes find an object

that does. Only rarely do we find an item that is museum worthy," Sikes said.

When they do find an item out of the realm of their expertise, they can tap an arsenal of experts in such areas as coins,
cars, antiques, jewelry, sports memorabilia, and more. They can
also use their network to market to collectors worldwide. (We'll
talk more about dealing with valuable items in Part Four.)

"What a relief for their kids!" I said, remembering how when
clearing out my parents' home I worried that I would sell a
Winslow Homer for five dollars.

"The number one wish people downsizing have is that they
want the items they love to go to those who will appreciate
them," said Sikes, echoing what I've heard my readers tell me
for years.

"And it's never their kids," I said.

"When family members don't share the same appreciation,
we find people who do," he said.

In Part Four of this book, we'll look at a variety of ways collectors can make sure their prized possessions go off to a good
home, but for now, here are a few opening thoughts.

Dos and Don'ts of Donating to the Arts

For downsizers or estate planners who want their valuables to fall into the right hands and their assets to support a good cause, Sikes and Fox offer these dos and don'ts:

DON'T

- **Do nothing.** Although inertia is the common default when faced with a houseful of stuff, not planning for the disposition of your treasured belongings ensures that someone who probably cares less than you do will.

- **Put it in storage.** Pleeeeeeeze do not pay to store your stuff. If you can't comfortably live in your home with what you have, sell or donate what you don't have room for. The United States has about fifty-three thousand storage facilities, according to the Self-Storage Association. That is more than all the Starbucks, McDonald's, and Subways combined. More than 90 percent of these storage facilities are full. The rest of the world has only about ten thousand storage facilities. This is an unconscionable waste of money and resources. And don't even get me started on the number of people who can't park even one car in their garage (one in four).

- **Leave it to the museum without asking.** When drawing up their will, some people stipulate that they want all their artwork and antiques to go to the museum without ever asking the museum, Sikes said. They think they're being charitable, but they put a terrible burden on the museum. The museum inherits all this stuff it didn't want. Permanent collections are a liability. They cost money to insure, store, and maintain.

DO

- **Ask your kids or other loved ones if they want anything of yours.** If they say they don't, believe them. If they do want an item, either give it to them right then or spell it out in the will so no one fights over it later.

- **Tell your story.** If an item has a great story, write it down and be sure the documentation is conveyed with the piece. One way to do that is to simply tape an envelope to the back of the item with a note inside explaining the provenance of the piece and how it came to you. (You'll read about a great example of this in chapter 20.) That will add not only to its value, but also to the new owner's appreciation.

- **Get an appraisal.** If you believe you have something of value, get it appraised by a specialist in that field. To find such an expert, search online for "certified appraiser," then look for one who specializes in what you're to have appraised, such as European antiques, clocks, old cars, or fine jewelry. (See Part Four for more examples of appraisals and working with appraisers.) Another option is to call an area auction house or furniture consignment store for a recommendation. Either way, an appraisal will help you prove authenticity and value if you sell it. If you donate the item, an appraisal will help you support the tax write-off. If you leave the item in your will to a family member, say an antique oil painting for your daughter, you can account for its value when you leave something of equivalent value, say a collection of rare arrowheads, to your son.

- **Donate without strings.** Museums used to get into a bind by promising donors they would always keep a piece on display, or that they would never break up a collection even if they only wanted one piece, Fox said. They got stuck holding these items into perpetuity. Today most museums agree only to "unencumbered" donations. That way, they make no promise that an item will be on display. They also are not bound to keep it and may sell or trade it.

- **Find a good home.** If the museum declines your donation, your pieces can still benefit the museum if you sell them and donate the proceeds. Go through an auction house or an online auction liquidator. (See chapter 17 for information on finding an auction house or local liquidator; Everything but the House and MaxSold are two such companies with locations in multiple

cities.) Although you'll pay a commission, you have a good shot
of finding a buyer who will cherish the items. (You'll read more
about these liquidation options in Part Four.)

- **Give creative gifts.** While institutions don't want unsolicited
  items, some museums, universities, and even churches welcome
  preapproved gifts of art or antiques. Be sure to ask for the person
  who heads their foundation or handles such gifts. The institution
  can sell these items for cash. In the end, kids and museums really
  want the same thing. Most would rather have cash than stuff.

CHAPTER 6

All for Art's Sake

Virginia and Ed Fultz

Turns out that not having kids is a good way to save a bunch of money. Not that I would know. Besides, I wouldn't trade my kids for a bigger bank account—on most days.

Being childless can also be really good for the arts. Ask Virginia and Ed Fultz of Albuquerque. Fifteen years ago, the married art lovers decided to leave their entire estate to their local museum. That means everything—their house, car, investment portfolio, and considerable art collection—altogether worth a few million, give or take.

"If we'd had children, they would have been our priority," Virginia told me when I got the couple on the phone one afternoon to talk about their gift. "But that didn't happen, so we went in a different direction."

They put their money where their hearts are.

Virginia and Ed are one of those long-married couples who tell stories together. After telling part of a story, Ed will say, "Virginia, you tell the rest of it."

Ed and Virginia met as teenagers while attending West Texas State College. They were in biology lab together, and he helped her dissect a frog. They married during their junior year, fifty-five years ago. After college, they both taught high school in El Paso for ten years. He taught biology, and she, English.

"We didn't grow up in homes with art," Virginia said. "What we knew of art, we'd learned from books."

Born and raised in Borger, Texas, a little oil town in the panhandle, Ed grew up the son of a homemaker and a machinist. Virginia's parents ran a diner in Mississippi before moving to Texas. "My parents weren't poor, but we didn't have any money," she said. They did manage to pay for Virginia to take piano lessons, enabling her to earn money playing for the Rotary Club and get a music scholarship to help pay for college.

Virginia and Ed's love affair with art began in the summer of 1968. As teachers, they had summers off, and they made the most of that time by traveling. That particular summer, they spent three months visiting every country in Western Europe.

"We bought a used Fiat in Amsterdam, put ten thousand miles on it, and sold it at the end of the trip," Ed said.

"We did the Europe-on-five-dollars-a-day plan because it fit our teacher budget," Virginia added. They hit every major museum, and many minor ones.

"That first trip to Europe was so eye-opening," Ed said.

"It was like this grand feast," Virginia added.

Indeed, on their first visit to the Louvre in Paris, she recalled, "We could barely afford lunch there. Then the waiter brought over this lovely hors d'oeuvres tray and two glasses of wine that we couldn't afford. We looked around and saw this nicely dressed gentleman sitting nearby and knew it was from him."

Art patrons are a generous bunch. Virginia and Ed are paying those moments forward.

Ed eventually left teaching and took a management job with a trucking company. In 1981 he was transferred to Albuquerque, a city he and his wife loved for its art and culture. Because it was August, no teaching positions were available, so Virginia got her broker's license and started selling real estate. "That career was quite wonderful to me."

After twenty years with the trucking company, Ed retired at age fifty-five and joined his wife in selling real estate. They continued to travel and have visited New Zealand, Australia, Singapore, Hong Kong, Ecuador, Iceland, and, of course, Europe and Mexico many times.

"Every time we traveled, we increased our love of art and our appreciation for the important place museums hold in every society. They enrich our lives," Ed said.

Today their large (and growing) collection includes pieces from a variety of countries, and many from their native Southwest.

"We don't buy what someone else likes," Ed said. "We buy what we love. It doesn't have to have value, nor do we need to think it will become valuable," although some of their pieces are by artists who have since become known.

"That's one of the traits that's so wonderful about them," said Emily Blaugrund Fox, the museum foundation director. "They not only collect art purely because they like a piece but also because they like an artist they meet and want to support him or her and have a memory of the meeting."

Like the taxi driver they met in Juárez, Mexico, who, while waiting for his next fare, would open the trunk of his car to sell his paintings. "He often drove us over the border from El Paso, and we loved that he was a cab driver and an artist. "We bought this crazy modern painting of a dancing girl, who turned out to be his daughter," Virginia said.

As for whether any of their art will wind up in the museum, the Fultzes have no expectations. Although the Albuquerque Museum has first dibs, "If they say they don't want anything, we will not be offended," Virginia said. "We have gotten our enjoyment."

Once the Albuquerque Museum passes, other museums in the area can have their pick, and after that, everything left will be sold, with the proceeds going to the museum foundation.

Meanwhile, the couple continues to appreciate their local museum's collection. "We often go and spend a couple of hours, have lunch and a glass of wine at the café and talk about art. It's a comfortable place for us," Virginia said. "Every time I go, it thrills me to know they will benefit from us someday. They've given us so much more than we'll ever give them."

"My hope is that someone enters the museum years after I'm gone and is able to enjoy just one piece of art our funds allowed the museum to purchase," Ed said. "I want to give someone else the same pleasure the museum has provided for me over the years, and help others learn to enjoy art and appreciate art."

"I don't feel the need for recognition or fame," Virginia added. "I'm just glad we can give back."

To prepare their art collection for the ultimate handoff, when items will either go to a museum or be sold for cash, the Fultzes have an art file. Each piece of artwork has a folder that includes information about the artist and the art itself, the sales receipt, and the story behind how they got it.

"The problem is, we have to quit collecting," Virginia said.

"That's not going to happen," Ed said.

"We are so behind on our files."

"If you saw our walls, you would laugh."

"Truly, we are not allowed to go to an art show for a year."

"We're going to one next week."

For now, Ed and Virginia, who are seventy-seven and seventy-six respectively, are still busy living, and not in any hurry to downsize. "We know we have too much stuff, but we are enjoying our life, our art, and our home. We don't want to live in an empty house," Virginia said.

However, it was the loss of their parents in the 1990s that prompted them to make an estate plan. "After clearing out and closing up their homes, we started thinking, *How should we do this?*" Ed said. Since they didn't have children, or any relatives interested in art or in need, they asked themselves what mattered.

"Most people are going to have children and grandchildren, so they will be in a different situation," Virginia said. "But those in situations like ours should think about the different experiences that have enriched their lives, whether it's been the theater, the library, their university, a sports program, or causes they believe need support, such as food banks, the church, or a charity that holds a special meaning, then look for a way to give to that institution. For us, loving art the way we do, it was easy. A culture devoid of art would be so tragic."

No garage sales

Deciding to leave your estate to a cause you love is step one. The next challenge, the Fultzes found, becomes *how*. "We didn't know where to go to find someone who could dispose of our art thoughtfully. That isn't so easy," Ed said. "Friends our age who are also collectors tell us their children aren't interested."

They knew they didn't want a relative to do the job. "We did not want to inconvenience our nieces and nephews or cause any infighting," he said. Initially, the Fultzes asked a younger friend to handle their estate. But that relationship soured. "You never think that a relationship will change, but in life they do," Ed said.

Next, they asked Fox if she would do the honors, so all the money could go to the museum. However, that posed a conflict, Fox said. "We need the separation in case the family has questions later. We can't open the museum to liability."

"We would have liked to have had the museum foundation act as our personal representative; then we would not have to pay a percentage to the trust company, and all [the money] could go to the museum, but, as Emily explained, the foundation was not in a position to do that," Ed said.

> *"A culture devoid of art would be so tragic."*
> —**Virginia Fultz**

Ultimately, the Fultzes hired a well-established trust company. For a percentage of the estate, the company will handle the sale of the art and other assets and disburse the proceeds.

"It's expensive, but worth it," Ed said. Their attorney agreed.

They interviewed the company's owner and explained that what mattered to them was that whoever handled the disposition of their art did so thoughtfully.

"We wanted to make sure the trust company wouldn't just sell all our art in a yard sale," Ed said. "We met with the owner, whose company came highly recommended, and he said, 'Believe me, your art collection is not going to be sold in a garage sale.' He told us how he sold art and that made us feel better."

To simplify matters further, they consolidated all of their finances into one mutual fund, again putting the museum foundation in second position, after each other. While they were at it, they arranged to be cremated and prepaid for that. The trust company has all the instructions.

The Foundation of Giving

Here's what Virginia and Ed learned as they went through the planning process:

- **Name the right entity.** When the Fultzes first drew up their will in 2005, they named the Albuquerque Museum as their second **beneficiary**, after each other. But in 2018 they met Emily Blaugrund Fox, executive director for the museum foundation, who explained that they should name the Albuquerque Museum *Foundation* as beneficiary, not the museum itself.

    "Most people don't know that if they write a check for one hundred dollars to the Albuquerque Museum that it's going to the city. Our museum is a city museum," Fox said. The art collection belongs to the city, and the staff are city employees.

    Thus, if someone leaves their art collection to the museum, "the city could fire sale it to get the money and not treat the donation with the same love and attention the museum foundation would," she said. "Our foundation's entire purpose is to support this particular museum. If you make it clear your gift is to the foundation, the city can't touch it."

    "We didn't want some city mayor to use the money for another project," said Ed, who adjusted the will accordingly. This can also be true of state-run museums and other government-owned institutions, such as colleges and some hospitals. Foundations are better positioned to manage donations.

    The lesson is to always inquire about the organization's foundation and to not donate directly to the organization itself. Colleges and universities are good examples. Most have foundations established to handle donations. Ask to speak to whoever heads the foundation or is in charge of gifts.

- **Don't do it alone.** Work with an attorney to make sure your will conveys what you intend and is valid under your state's laws. An attorney can also be sure your will spells out exactly what you want to leave and to whom, lists all assets, and names the executor. (More on wills in chapter 11.)

- **Be specific.** Make clear how you want your gift to be used. The Fultzes earmarked their donation for art acquisitions. "Others may designate their funds to support exhibitions, capital improvement, or education," Fox said, "but don't restrict the gift too much. Gifts that come with strings can be difficult to honor."

- **Find a trustworthy representative.** Naming your executor—or personal representative, as they're called in some states—is a pivotal choice. Although most people appoint a family member for this role, a corporate **trustee** who works for a large financial institution like Charles Schwab or Fidelity may be a safer bet. Estate attorneys often find themselves needing to remove family members from positions of trust. You also want to make sure this individual is not in a position to access all the funds with no accountability. As you will see later, when large sums of money are at stake, even loving, kind family members can change.

- **Tell the recipient.** Do let whomever you're leaving an asset to know you've named them in your will, said Fox. Be sure they want it. Many donors don't tell organization leaders they've left money or other assets to the institution because they want to stay under the radar, she said. They don't want people to know, and they don't want to be pestered. In that case, Fox advises donors to simply tell the foundation they want to be left alone. "They will respect that, but do make your plans known."

CHAPTER 7

Remember Where You Came From

Paying homage to home

Brian Fogle was getting ready for a press conference the day I got him on the phone. He was announcing a $12 million gift that Linda Hale, a former longtime resident of Sheldon, Missouri, had left to the Community Foundation of the Ozarks and to Missouri State University to share. Each organization was to receive $6 million.

While that is not an everyday donation for the foundation, don't let the coveralls and flannel shirts fool you. The money may come in smaller doses from farms and sawmills, but wealth in the rural southern half of Missouri around Springfield is not as rare as some might think, Fogle assured me.

"Rural folks just aren't flashy with their money. They don't want to be pretentious," he said. As the president and CEO of the Ozarks community foundation, Fogle's job is to understand the core of his community—what makes it tick. And he does.

A feisty group of Scots and Irish who came from the Carolinas and Tennessee settled in the Ozarks in the early 1800s. "People didn't move to the Ozarks to join the Rotary," he said. "These people were an independent sort, and that spirit has lasted."

Because the region is blessed with natural beauty and great lakes, rivers, and streams, it draws outdoor enthusiasts who come to vacation. Meanwhile, its low cost of living draws retirees from the north looking to escape harsher winters. The problem is that that doesn't stop the outward migration of younger residents who want to leave rural life behind.

"Our challenge," Fogle shared, "is that kids aren't staying on the farm so much anymore." When they grow up and move away, their money and whatever they inherit goes with them, unless families deliberately leave a legacy behind. That's what Fogle tries to encourage.

The role of the community foundation

More than 750 community foundations operate in urban and rural areas in every state in the United States, according to the Council on Foundations. In 2019, the Community Foundation of the Ozarks ranked seventieth in terms of assets, with $300 million in managed funds. It ranks sixth busiest in number of transactions. By comparison, the Ozarks foundation's average gift is one-tenth the size of the average gift to Tulsa's community foundation, the second-largest one in the nation with $4 billion in assets.

Where Does the Money Go?

Typically, gifts that flow through community foundations go to religious organizations first, followed by education, then health care. Animals and the environment fall near the bottom of the giving hierarchy. In 2018, Americans gave $428 billion in charitable donations, about 2 percent of the nation's gross domestic product. The charitable giving came from these sources:

- 68% private individuals
- 18% foundations
- 9% bequests
- 5% corporations

Here's where it went:

- 29% religion
- 14% education
- 12% human services/relief efforts
- 12% gifts to grantmaking foundations
- 10% health
- 7% public-society benefit
- 5% arts, culture, and the humanities
- 5% international affairs
- 3% environment/animals
- 2% individuals
- 1% unallocated giving

Source: Giving USA, the longest-running annual report on US charitable giving

Although community foundations have different cultures, most share this singular appeal: As adults age and consider their legacy, many want to pay homage to the place that gave them their start.

Maybe that place is where they were born, or where they grew up. Maybe it's where they went to school, raised a family, made a home, or vacationed. Maybe it's where they found their calling and built their career. Wherever and for whatever reason, connection to place is a powerful force. So much so that leaving a legacy to a place is the third most common form of giving, after religious causes and education, Fogle said. What defines a community foundation gift is that they are place based and fit into the needs of the community.

Those needs can vary widely. The needs in the Ozarks, for instance, are vastly different from those in the Bay Area. "Our local boards have a much better idea of what our community needs than federal legislators."

That discernment, combined with the desire many have to honor their love of home and place, are what make the community foundation model so successful.

Serving fifty-eight counties in the southern half of Missouri, which includes the rural Ozarks, the foundation has 3,500 separate charitable funds. A donor may open a fund with $2,500 or more, naming anyone or any cause. "We can direct funds to go wherever the donor wants, so long as it's legal," Fogle said. And they do get creative.

For instance, when Tom Finnie, Springfield's longtime city manager, retired at age sixty-five, he insisted he did not want a party or a dinner or any fanfare. "If there was one, I wouldn't show up," Finnie said.

So Fogle, the mayor, and the head of the local chamber of commerce came up with a different idea. They raised $30,000 for an **endowment** in Finnie's name.

"I couldn't change their minds at that point," Finnie said. "It was a fait accompli."

The gesture became a turning point in Finnie's life. "I worked for city government for forty years. I am by no means a rich person. But now I had a sum of money I could direct." The idea also spawned a way for the city to recognize future public officials as they retired.

He matched the endowment with $30,000 of his own money and directed that the funds go to his two pet causes: the Springfield Botanical Gardens and Sister Cities International. A master gardener, Finnie has spent much of his time volunteering at the local botanical gardens. When his wife died five years after the endowment was formed, he established the Kay Cummins Finnie Dogwood Garden in honor of her favorite tree.

Leaving a legacy to a place is the third most common form of giving, after religious causes and education.

While working as a city manager, he grew to appreciate the work of Sister Cities, a nonprofit that creates partnerships between communities in the United States and those in other countries. "I know of many good causes in this world, but I found that, for me, focusing on two that I was actively involved in gave me the most joy."

In addition to scholarships and faith-oriented funds and gifts designated for a certain charity, such as the local food bank or hospital, the foundation also has field-of-interest funds. If someone loves the arts but doesn't want to leave money to just one arts organization, they can leave it to the general arts fund. Although types of funds vary widely, their common denominator is that they all funnel back into the community.

Cash or gift card?

Like every foundation director, the gifts Fogle likes most are unrestricted gifts. Unrestricted gifts are to fund-specific gifts what cash is to a store gift card. "Unrestricted gifts let us be most responsive to community needs," he said. "For instance, who would have foreseen the meth-and-opioid crisis becoming such a big deal here? Those unrestricted dollars gave us the means to respond to that need. But we understand that people have passions and want to fund specific causes."

He also knows his customers. They place a high value on financial security and privacy. "They are a generation of savers. They are generous when they die, but don't like to give while they're living. They worry they will run out of money; they worry about paying for the nursing home," he said. "And they shy away from the limelight."

They are humble, salt-of-the-earth types who don't want attention. When Fogle reaches out to the organization his donors want to support, he's often obliged to keep their gift quiet.

Some want their gifts anonymous during their life, but will allow their name to be mentioned afterward, like Linda and Larry Hale.

After meeting at and graduating from Missouri State University, the Hales returned to their small town of Sheldon, Missouri, where they worked for forty years in real estate and cattle ranching. "The Hales left their small community to seek an education, then returned to put that gift of learning toward building a life," Fogle said. "It's the American story."

They so loved their town and their alma mater that upon their death they left $12 million total to both organizations. Linda died three years after her husband, at which time the trust transferred the gift from her estate. Both the gift to the university and the community will fund scholarships for students in the counties near where the Hales lived and worked.

"So often we think of generational wealth," Fogle said, "but many of our wealthier community members, like the Hales, are self-made. Their gift will provide that same opportunity for other students. It's a legacy that will go on forever."

A little can go a long way

While the Hale gift is especially large, gifts to the community foundation come in all sizes. Fogle told me about a schoolteacher from Mountain Grove, Missouri, who never married and had no children. She owned a small house worth $65,000, which she left in her will to the community.

Proceeds from the home's sale went to create an endowment, which the foundation invested. Over time the investment fund grew to more than $100,000. Now the interest earnings pay for one or two scholarships a year, which is just what the schoolteacher wanted. "Her gift is changing the trajectory of students' lives," Fogle said.

"A donation like that is a big gift in a community like ours, while it would be far less impactful if she'd donated her house to, say, the American Cancer Society," he said. "Because we're small, every gift matters. I've given rural grants out to mayors who literally started crying when they got a five-thousand-dollar check for their communities. In big cities, that wouldn't even register."

How foundations manage their money

For anyone interested in leaving a gift to their community foundation, here's how it works. About 80 percent of all planned giving comes through simple wills and bequests, Fogle said. That is, people name the foundation in their will and say they want to leave a specific amount or a percentage of their estate to the foundation. Donors can specify their wishes in their wills or trusts in straightforward language, such as: "Upon my passing, I leave X percent of my estate to the Community Foundation of the Ozarks to be used as a scholarship fund." Or they can name the foundation as a beneficiary of a retirement account or life-insurance policy.

Whatever the case, Fogle and his team work with professional advisers, including accountants and attorneys, to make the arrangements for those clients who want to give back to their community. "Most of our planned giving work comes through professional advisers, who'll call and say, 'We have a client who really wants to help children.' We point them to the charities in the community that serve those needs."

From the money it manages on behalf of donors, the foundation keeps about 1 percent to cover its overhead. To keep the endowment growing, they invest it. Those who invest endowment funds do so with a different optic than the rest of us. Unlike a retirement fund, endowments don't have an endpoint. They are invested for perpetuity. A typical foundation invests funds in a diversified way to protect against market volatility. Typical vehicles for growth include stocks, hedge funds, and fixed-income funds. "We'll never outperform in a bull market, but will always do better than most in a bear market," Fogle said.

Even if the foundation makes only a 1.5 percent return, they take a percent and still have half a percent growth to give back to the endowment.

Some donors start giving through their community foundations before they die through a **designated fund**, an arrangement in which a donor gives a financial gift that the foundation will manage and use to support charities of the donor's choice. This lets the donor see their gift working in the community while they're alive. "On the donor's behalf, we may disburse several checks a year to the donor's favorite charities," Fogle said. These designated funds can continue to disburse funds to those causes long after a donor dies.

The power of variance

One concern donors often have is what happens if the organization they've chosen to support either changes its mission to one they wouldn't support or closes altogether after the donor has died. Say, for instance, you left a substantial gift to a women's college that later began to accept men.

Because such changes do happen, foundations and other nonprofit organizations have what's called a **power of variance.** If a designated charity changes its direction and is no longer aligned with the deceased donor's wish, most organizations can adapt using this tool and redirect the funds.

Fogle recalls an instance when the local organization to help the blind closed its doors. The foundation found a similar cause and redirected the funds its donors had earmarked for that defunct organization to the comparable cause to help the blind. The power of variance would also kick in if a church you wanted to support dissolved. In that case, the foundation would have to find a church close by of a similar denomination and mission.

Trickier to address are cases where an organization changes its mission. Let's say a group you supported that was once pro-environment suddenly came out saying climate change was a hoax. In these cases, if the family fund has a successor adviser, a person the donor appointed to make decisions after they die, the successor can shift the money elsewhere.

If the same organization had a change of leadership, programming, or mission, the successor adviser would work to reallocate the money. For instance, if I were to leave an endowment to my alma mater, the University of Kansas School of Journalism, and the university closed the J-school, the gift might then go to endow the professor teaching journalism in KU's English Department.

However, Fogle warns, matters involving donor intent aren't always so clean. After a donor dies, proving his or her intent when things change is difficult if not impossible. Lawsuits have arisen over such issues. He recalls one case closely watched by charitable organizations in which the heirs of donors Charles and Marie Robertson, who had given $35 million to Princeton University in 1961 to prepare men and women for careers in government services geared toward international affairs, claimed the school had changed its direction and violated the terms of the donation and the gift's intent. The heirs argued that rather than train students to work for government, Princeton had turned the program into a factory for business students. Princeton argued that times had changed, and so had the need.

After an expensive six-year lawsuit, the parties settled in 2008. The family gave up its role at the school. Princeton kept most of the funds in the endowment, which had grown to $900 million before the recession, and paid the family nearly $100 million. The heirs planned to use the funds to start a new foundation to train students for government careers.

Seven Options for Planned Giving

Donors who want to make a planned gift through their community foundations, or to other nonprofits, have a variety of options. These planned gifts can have a beneficial impact on estate and income taxes for you and your heirs. Ask your advisers about the best assets to donate as well as the optimal timing of your gifts.

1. Name a charity in your will and specify a dollar amount or percentage you wish to leave. If you want your gift to be used in a specific way, discuss that with an adviser from the charity to make sure.

2. Designate an asset (car, boat, savings or checking account, etc.) that is to go to a charity, and make the asset payable on death (POD) or transferable on death (TOD) to the charity.

3. Name a charity as a life-insurance beneficiary.

4. Name a charity as a beneficiary of an IRA or other retirement account.

5. Name one or several charities as beneficiaries of a donor-advised fund.

6. Gift real estate or other appreciated assets outright or upon death. (If you plan to donate your home, talk to your adviser about a charitable life estate, which allows you to continue living in your home after you donate it.

7. Make a charitable gift part of the sale of a business. You can also give publicly traded stock to a charity. These direct donation strategies can reduce your taxes more than if you sell the business or stock first, then make gifts from the proceeds of the sale.

Source: National Association of Charitable Gift Planners

Giving in the Extreme

Just as we've found that no gift is too small, apparently none is too big, either. If you ever have a day when your faith in humanity has waned to a nadir, look up stories about the Giving Pledge (givingpledge.org). An effort to help solve the world's biggest problems through giving, the Giving Pledge invites those of extreme wealth—one has to have a net worth of $1 billion or more—to commit more than half their wealth to philanthropy or charitable causes during their lifetime or in their wills.

Created in 2010 by Bill and Melinda Gates and Warren Buffett, who together wanted to set a new standard of generosity among others in their financial stratosphere, the movement has attracted more than two hundred members worldwide, Elon Musk and Mark Zuckerberg among them.

Members support a wide range of issues including poverty allevi-ation, refugee aid, disaster relief, global health, education, medical research, criminal justice reform, environmental sustainability, and arts and culture.

By setting a high bar, and a heartwarming example, members hope to shift the social norms of giving and inspire everyone to give more, to establish their giving plans sooner, and to give in smarter ways. Now, that's something to aspire to.

CHAPTER 8

Paying It Back & Paying It Forward

For some, leaving a legacy begins now

O f course, you don't have to wait until you die to create your legacy. Though earmarking where your money will go in an estate plan is a practical imperative, in fact, many passionate philanthropists create their legacies while in the prime of life.

Cindy Lopez of Los Angeles and Kim Trent of Detroit are examples. Helping those who have less access to education—either due to their socioeconomic status, family situations, or race—break through barriers has become their calling. Although both women came from families that expected them to go to college, what they saw when they got there drove them to help smooth the way for those coming behind them.

Cindy Lopez—making the legacy leap

Cindy Lopez remembers the moment she wanted to become a lawyer. It was the 1970s. She was in seventh grade and saw a TV show that featured a female attorney. "I thought to myself, *Wow! That's so cool. I want to do that!*"

The only problem was that she didn't know any lawyers. She wouldn't meet one for ten years. The oldest of three girls, she and her sisters lived in Anaheim, California, with their mom, who was born in the Dominican Republic and never went to college.

Despite not having role models, Lopez figured it out. After working for thirty-three years as a prosecutor, she now works to help under-resourced students of color get into the practice of law. She aims not only to help them but also to help her profession by bringing in more diversity. While working as a deputy attorney general for the California Attorney General's Office, she also served for twenty years on the board of MOSTe (Motivating Our Students Through Experience), a community-based mentoring, scholarship, and college-access organization that encourages young women from underserved areas of Los Angeles County to become the first generation in their families go to college.

"I saw how an organization like that could completely change the trajectory of a student's life," she said. When she retired in 2019 at age fifty-nine, she wanted to do more, and so she founded LEAP—Legal Education Access Pipeline—a nonprofit mentoring program that helps those underrepresented in the legal community to more easily clear the hurdles that stand between them, law school, and a successful legal career.

"I started LEAP because when I applied to law school, I had literally no help," Lopez said. "I went in blind. I want these students to have a different experience. I want them to talk to attorneys, ask them about their career options and their lifestyles."

She also wants to help "create a legal landscape that reflects the diversity of our communities," she said. "A more diverse legal community is a more just community. I want these students not just to practice law but to serve on the bench. We need diversity where decisions are being made."

LEAP is open to college students or recent college graduates who are planning to apply to law school and who fall into at least one of the following groups: They are of color, have low socioeconomic status, are first-generation college students, or identify as LGBTQ (lesbian, gay, bisexual, transgender, and queer or questioning). Most fall into at least two of those categories, she said.

When I spoke with Lopez, LEAP was turning two. She sounded like a proud parent. In its first year, fifty-seven students applied to the program and thirty-one were accepted. Of those, sixteen applied to law school and all but one got in. The second year, 190 students applied to LEAP; 46 were accepted. "It's become ridiculously competitive," she said.

LEAP's funding comes from law firms, companies, private donors, and soon, Lopez hopes, from planned giving. "That's my next development phase," she said. "I want to coach donors to leave a legacy gift to LEAP in their wills."

The group of donors she's targeting includes herself: "I haven't created my will or trust yet, and I need to," she said, conceding that, as a lawyer, she knows better. Though Lopez is single and has no children, "I have property and causes I want to support, like LEAP," she said. "It's time I took care of this."

Kim Trent—channeling Rosa Parks

Like Cindy Lopez, Kim Trent shares the philosophy that lifting up others of color becomes a calling for those who have made it. "I live in a city where a lot of people don't have opportunity," said the lifelong Detroit resident. "Regardless of your economic status, you cannot grow up in Detroit and not see how inequity has shaped our reality."

Although Trent came from a middle-class family and was expected to go to college, she feels "a great deal of responsibility to open doors for others who didn't have the opportunities I had," she said. One of those opportunities was a full-ride scholarship to Wayne State University, which she received in 1987 from the Rosa L. Parks Scholarship Foundation.

Established in 1980 through fundraising efforts led by the Detroit Public Schools and *The Detroit News*, the Rosa Parks Foundation recognizes top Michigan high school students who demonstrate a financial need and an interest in social justice.

When Trent won her scholarship, *The Detroit News* was looking to recruit more people of color into its newsroom. The newspaper worked with the foundation to offer a full scholarship to a student wanting to major in journalism, which Trent did. She also got to work as an intern at the paper and landed a reporting job there when she graduated.

"I remember being so excited to have my name associated with Mrs. Parks. I consider it one of my great blessings in life that I had the opportunity to escort her to a scholarship luncheon." Rosa Parks became an icon of the civil rights movement when, in 1955, in Montgomery, Alabama, she refused to give her bus seat to a white passenger, triggering protests across America. She died in 2005.

As president, Trent keeps Parks's legacy alive by working to grow the dwindling endowment through fundraising, so it can continue to meet its current goal of offering smaller one-time scholarships ($2,000) to forty students per year. "Rosa wanted to give young people who had a desire to serve an opportunity to have an education."

And so does Trent.

Today, Trent also serves as deputy director for prosperity for Michigan's Department of Labor and Economic Opportunity. "I passionately believe, and the research bears this out, there is no better anti-poverty strategy than a four-year degree."

Like her predecessor, Trent—who is fifty-two, married, and has a thirteen-year-old son—plans to leave her own legacy. Beyond making a difference in Black lives while she's alive, she will leave money behind for those causes she's invested in. "The Rosa Parks Scholarship Foundation and Wayne State are definitely on the list," she said.

The efforts of Lopez and Trent are wonderful examples of how people with purpose and passion can create a legacy while they're alive that will have ripple effects for years to come. As the common fundraising refrain goes: Whether you give your time, talent, or treasure, all gifts are welcome. Fortunately for those whose lives have changed as a result, some donors give all the above.

Gloria Galanes—helping the offbeat

When Dr. Gloria Galanes first got asked to serve on the board of the Community of the Ozarks Foundation, she thought the caller had the wrong number.

"Isn't that for people who have a lot of money?" the retired college professor asked, because that wasn't her.

"Actually, we're looking for people who can think through issues," the caller said. One of those issues was how to respond to a foundation-commissioned study of wealth in Springfield, which found that the greatest transfer of wealth in the country's history was about to happen, and as it did, a lot of wealth was bound to leave the community—unless the foundation did something.

Galanes did serve on the board for six years, and became part of the team that came up with the 5 percent campaign: *Take care of your family. Take care of your church, but consider leaving 5 percent of your assets to where you came from.*

The more involved Galanes got, the more she began to question what mattered to her. What became clear to the lifelong educator was what education had meant to her, and what it had done for her family.

Galanes's four grandparents had all emigrated from Greece. None had a formal education, and only one knew how to read and write. Her father, a chemical engineer, and his five siblings had all gone to college, the first generation in her family to do so. That formal education forever changed the trajectory of this poor, immigrant family.

Years later, Galanes earned not only a four-year degree from the University of Michigan but also her doctorate from

Ohio State University. She began her career at Missouri State University in 1986, where she taught organizational leadership and communications, and eventually became dean of the Judith Enyeart Reynolds College of Arts and Letters there. She retired in 2017 at age seventy, in better financial shape than she expected.

"In my twenties I thought, *If I'm going to have a career in academia, I'm going to be a bag lady*." The thought sufficiently scared her, so she started putting money away in a 403(b) account—like a 401(k), but for public employees and some others. The university contributed to her defined benefit retirement plan, or pension. Careful living and that steady contribution ultimately added up to a $1 million nest egg. She lives comfortably on what she receives each month from Social Security and her university pension.

Although well set, Galanes, who's divorced with no children, does not consider herself rich. She and her partner of thirty years "don't live extravagantly," she said.

Serving on the community foundation board, however, got her thinking about what was meaningful to her, and how she could pay that forward. The answer was clear: Education was number one.

She worked with a financial adviser, an attorney, and a tax adviser to create her estate plan, which includes a will and a trust. As her campaign suggested, her plan earmarks 5 percent of her assets for the Missouri State University Foundation when she dies. She's designated half of her donation to help fund tuition for kids attending the Missouri Fine Arts Academy, a two-week program at the university for high school juniors and seniors.

"Missouri is very conservative. These kids often come from rural areas. It's critically important to me that these artistic kids, who are often a little offbeat and therefore bullied and misunderstood, can come to a program like this and finally see other kids like them, and see a future."

The other half will go to an animal fund she established through the community foundation. "I don't decide where the money goes, but I know the foundation will do what's best with it to help animals find homes."

The remainder of her estate will go to her partner, Noah. If he dies before her, her younger sister is next in line. She keeps all of her important papers—her will, trust documents, birth certificate, credit card information, real estate papers, and bank account and pension plan information—in a binder, and she updates her plan every five years.

"Here all along I thought that this sort of giving was just for rich people. It's not. Beyond that, it's a relief to know all is taken care of, and I'm taken care of. Now I just get to live my life."

Tom Finnie—the importance of purpose

For retired people, having a purpose in life can be "a big damn problem," Tom Finnie told me one afternoon when I caught him on the phone. "You go from being somebody to being nobody, and wondering, *Why am I here?*"

Knowing that his identity would be at stake, when the former city manager transitioned into retirement, he made a point to look around at those who were happily retired and ask how they did it. "What I saw was they all had some passion they moved into. And I knew I needed to find that."

The endowment his contemporaries formed in his name kickstarted him into identifying his twin passions: the local botanical gardens and the Sister Cities initiative, causes he doesn't just financially support, but also physically supports. "I'm seventy-nine years old and carry shovels and rakes to the gardens to work."

In addition to having a passion, Finnie says two more ingredients are necessary for a happy retirement. "Having friends is one, and you can't have friends if you're not happy, and a fair supply of bourbon is the other."

A good financial plan matters, too.

In addition to his planned-giving funds, Finnie also has a will, a trust, and an end-of-life plan. "They are all intertwined," Finnie said. His family knows what they all entail.

"A will should not just be a checklist flung on your family after you're dead, but something your family agrees to," he said. "I've seen too many families torn up because their parents didn't talk about their end-of-life plan. Maybe it's inertia, or maybe it seems too complicated, or maybe they're afraid the kids won't like their idea. Regardless, families need to talk about their wills or trusts so the news doesn't come as a surprise. I didn't want my family to deal with a mess."

Following in his father's footsteps

Fortunately, Finnie had a good role model. He learned about generosity and communicating plans for giving from his father. The first in his family to go to college, his dad graduated from the University of Kentucky College of Engineering and went on to work for the US Department of Defense.

Before he died, he told Tom and his brother that if it were OK with them, he wanted to leave a $500,000 endowment to his engineering school to fund scholarships for students who were also the first in their families to go to engineering school.

"I remember going to events at the university where my father was thanked, and how very meaningful that was to him," Finnie said. Today the engineering fund keeps giving, and Finnie and his brother don't have to do a thing.

"Once a year we get a nice letter from students," he said.

Now, Finnie is carrying on his father's legacy of giving and leaving an example for his two grown children. They appreciate the legacy their dad has left them. Plus, they enjoy another benefit of their dad's planned fund. Instead of getting frustrated trying to come up with a present for him for Christmas or his birthday, they just donate to his fund.

"Everyone wins, and the community foundation makes this easy," Finnie said.

To keep his affairs organized and in order, all of his assets—the house, stocks, other investments—are in one trust. His kids know where the binder is that holds copies of his investments, retirement plan, and advance directive. "They both know I don't want to be rescued."

And they know the plan: Finnie has left 10 percent of his estate (an endowment of around $100,000) to his two causes, and the remainder will be split between his son and daughter. "My kids won't have to make any decisions after I die."

He plans, however, to take the bourbon with him.

CHAPTER 9

A Gift for the Generations

Arlene Cogen

Like many financial types, Arlene Cogen, a certified financial planner from Portland, Oregon, never thought much about leaving her own legacy until the opportunity hit home.

Ten years ago, Cogen's mother learned she had pancreatic cancer and six to eight months to live. The slightly silver lining in this sad news was that this gave Cogen and her two older siblings time to be with their mom, and to have those meaningful last conversations. They took turns staying with their mom, a widow for more than a decade.

"My mother and I had the most beautiful discussions," Cogen told me. At one point, her mother asked Cogen to review her estate plan. After charity, the remaining assets were to be divided equally among the siblings. However, Cogen noticed that only 5 percent of her mother's estate was going to charity.

"We kids were all successful and didn't need the money, so I said, 'Why not make it 10 percent?'"

With her children's blessing, she did.

Then the fun began, Cogen said. "She was like a kid in a candy store deciding which charitable gifts to increase."

Among the more meaningful gifts she left was $25,000 to her synagogue, Congregation B'nai Torah of Ormond Beach, Florida. It was the largest gift her congregation had ever received. Part of that gift goes to fund the synagogue's Always Be Learning education scholarship, which her mother created.

"Mom was so filled with joy during the process, which was both beautiful and painful," Cogen said.

Finding the joy sooner

A former Wall Street executive, Cogen left the East Coast in 1999 and moved to Oregon, where she transitioned into the world of nonprofit development. During her nine years as the director of gift planning for the Oregon Community Foundation, consistently ranked among the US's top ten largest community foundations, she facilitated more than $96 million in charitable gifts.

While she worked with financial advisers who were helping clients give back through their estate plans, she saw that most people hang on to their assets while living in case they need them and leave the biggest gift they will ever make when they die. Halfway through her time with the community foundation, her mom died. And that's when Cogen's legacy began.

The experience changed how Cogen viewed charitable giving. Her kids now embrace that view, too. "In my work, I often met people who waited until the very end to experience the fun

> *Most people hang on to their assets while living in case they need them, and then leave the biggest gift they will ever make when they die.*

and fulfillment of philanthropy. I didn't want to be one of those people."

When Cogen's mother turned the lens on her daughter and asked her what she was going to do with her inheritance, the answer was easy: She would take her husband and two children to Israel so they could see the roots of their heritage, create a charitable fund and put the rest toward the education of her daughters, Abby and Alana.

The girls, who were then in their mid-teens, became part of the giving. The family created the Arlene and Mitch Cogen Family Fund through the Oregon Community Foundation with a gift of $25,000. The fund has no guidelines. Each year, the girls decide where the proceeds from the fund, usually around 5 percent, or $1,250, should go. Recently they picked Abby's Closet, a charity that helps get prom dresses for girls who otherwise can't afford them.

"We choose small organizations where our gift can have an impact," she said. "Every year we talk about where we want to give, and how we want to make a difference."

When Cogen's brother, Sam Siegel, died in 2019, the girls knew what to do. To honor their uncle, a self-described computer nerd, they created a science, technology, engineering, and math scholarship fund in his name to help young women get into those fields.

The Cogen fund is flexible "because I don't want to limit what I think is important," said Cogen, who nicknamed her fund "the Current Problem Fund." "Times change, so flexible giving is important."

A hundred years ago, when community funds were first established, a donor may have wanted to make sure every courthouse had a place to tie a horse up out front, and maybe now what matters is that the courthouse has a place to plug in an electric car. This is where the community fund's power of variance comes in.

As with the other financial experts and estate lawyers I talked to, Cogen confirmed that in her experience the percentage of people who leave money when they die to causes beyond their families is remarkably small. She's working to change that.

After leaving the foundation, Cogen started a consulting firm to help people make charitable gifts and wrote *Give to Live*, a book on charitable giving.

"I wanted to take the idea of philanthropy away from millionaires and make it accessible to everyone"—to people like her mom. "Mom never imagined she would ever be able to make that kind of a difference."

But she did.

Three Easy Ways to Give

"Most people do not give to charity because they think that's for millionaires, and they don't know how to include philanthropy in their plan," Arlene Cogen said. Many advisers don't have the tools or the time to bring clients through the process to show how accessible leaving a legacy truly is.

Whereas a professional adviser might help you avoid negatives like excess taxes, probate, creditors, and challengers to your will or trust, if you want to gain positive results from your plan, and give back in enriching ways, you will need to express that in your meetings with your adviser so that those wishes get incorporated into your planning. Here are three ways Cogen likes to help clients make a positive change.

- **Designate a charity as beneficiary.** Every retirement plan has a place to name a beneficiary, usually your spouse. But here is an opportunity to also leave a tax-free gift to charity.

  Tell your plan administrator to give a percentage of what's left in your retirement plan to a charity of your choice. For example, let's say when you die, you have $200,000 left in your IRA and your spouse is no longer alive. You want 80 percent of that ($160,000) divided evenly between your two children, and the remaining 20 percent ($40,000) to go to the American Wild Horse Campaign, to save wild horses from slaughterhouses. You can do that outside of a trust, and outside of probate. (For more on avoiding probate, see chapter 12.)

- **Create a charitable gift annuity.** Some, though not all, charities allow donors to create a charitable gift annuity, which is a way to make a charitable donation and get a guaranteed income while you're alive, or to give the annuity payment to others. The annual payments can be quite good for older people. Among the benefits of this type of gift is that, depending on the charity, you can start one with less money than you would need to start a charitable trust.

- **Give the gift you always give—forever.** Let's say that every year you give $100 to the same cause, like the Make-A-Wish Foundation of America, which benefits critically ill children. Now take that same amount and multiply it by twenty to get $2,000. If you leave a $2,000 planned gift to that charity through your estate plan either directly with the organization (if they are set up to create an endowment fund) or through a community foundation, if managed properly, that $2,000 endowment can continue to give your chosen charity $100 a year into perpetuity. It's that simple.

Choose Charities with Care

Not all charities are created equal. Many are wonderful, but, sadly, some are shams. Before you name one in your will, check it out. Be especially wary of soundalike charities, ones that sound worthy, but are fraudulent. Here are some sites that will serve as good starting points when searching for a worthwhile cause and learning more about how they operate, so you can make sure your money is going to a legitimate cause:

- Charity Navigator: charitynavigator.org
- Charity Watch: charitywatch.org
- The Better Business Bureau's Wise Giving Alliance: give.org
- Guidestar: guidestar.org

- **Look past the name.** Many charities' names sound philanthropic, but the name doesn't tell you the whole story. One cause to support the blind may be a hoax, while another may be legitimate. Some poorly run or even fraudulent charities have names that sound a lot like highly rated ones. For example, *Consumer Reports* set up a grading system to use when evaluating charities. In its 2019 report,* it gave the United Breast Cancer

Foundation of Huntington, New York, a low rating—and the Breast Cancer Research Foundation of New York City, a high rating. Pay attention not only to the charity's name, but also to its web address. Scammers often mimic the names of familiar, trusted organizations to fool donors.

- **Run a search.** Type in the charity's name plus the word "reviews," "complaints," or "scam" and see what surfaces. Or type in the kind of charity you want to support, such as animal welfare or clean water, and then "highly rated" to surface the good actors.

- **Check their numbers.** The best charities put most of their funds toward their cause and spend only a small amount on administrative costs (salaries and overhead) and fundraising. Use the websites above to look for charities that independent audits confirm spend 70 percent or more on their mission, and to see how different charities stack up.

- **Give directly.** Be sure your executor or the person handling your trust is donating directly to the organization and not through a "professional fundraiser," who might be keeping a portion.

---

*consumerreports.org/charities/best-charities-for-your-donations

Successful, Single, and Charitable

Carol Zurcher is a certified public accountant and personal financial specialist in her fifties. She never married or had children, but she is a fantastic sister and aunt. Zurcher, who practices in Winter Park, Florida, does what she tells her clients to do: She has created a plan that puts loved ones first, then also gives to charity. She has the bulk of her assets in a trust, and has named her mother, sister, niece, and nephew as beneficiaries. Separate from that she also has her own **charitable donor-advised fund,** which is more cost-effective than a private foundation, she said. She established the fund a few years ago solely for charitable giving.

The Compassionately Engaged Zurcher Foundation (which uses her initials but not her full name to provide some anonymity) is a donor-advised fund that she keeps with Charles Schwab. The fund lets her support causes she believes in—and manage her taxable income.

Assets that go into these funds are tax deductible and can grow tax-free.

Although Zurcher has wide latitude about where the money can go, one place it cannot go is back to her estate. In that respect, donor advised funds are irrevocable—once you put the money in, you may not take it out for your personal use. With a donor-advised fund, all the money in the fund must go fully to the beneficiaries—in this case, selected charities.

Since establishing the fund, Zurcher has donated money to the Gary Sinise Foundation for veterans, to mental health organizations that serve children, to her church, to animal causes, and to organizations working to promote racial equality.

"I give wherever I see a need," she said, adding that she gets to know the charities to ensure they really are fulfilling their stated mission. (See the previous box for a list of websites to help you do this.) For added protection, Charles Schwab also makes sure the money goes only to legitimate nonprofits.

When Zurcher dies, her appointed successor can select future causes to receive the remaining funds as she would have wanted. However, she's not expecting that day to come anytime soon. Knowing these funds are irrevocable, Zurcher has made sure to leave enough to take care of herself for her lifetime. "I'm planning for beyond a hundred just in case," she said.

CHAPTER 10

A Cautionary Tale

The Quinn family

The story of the Quinn family is a textbook example of good intentions gone bad. (I've changed the names in this true story to protect the family's privacy. I also corroborated the story through court documents.)

I first learned about the Quinns' case from Charlie Quinn. Charlie read my book *Downsizing the Family Home*, and after reading my section on sibling quarrels, he wrote to tell me that his sibling relations didn't end so well after his parents died.

Charlie was in his sixties when his parents both died in 2010, just a few months apart. Mr. and Mrs. Quinn were married for sixty-five years and had four children. They lived most of their lives in rural New England, where they led a nice but not extravagant life.

"We never had a fancy house or fancy cars and didn't take expensive trips," Charlie told me. His parents were frugal savers. By the time they both died at the age of ninety-one, they had assets of around $1.4 million. They also had a will simply stating that after the last spouse died, all the remaining assets would be divided equally among the four children.

Mr. and Mrs. Quinn took heart in knowing that thanks to their careful planning, each of their children, and in turn their grandchildren, would be taken care of, and that their frugal living would become a financial legacy that would extend to the next generation.

To make sure that happened, and to ensure that none of their hard-earned money was squandered, Mr. Quinn researched the worlds of estates, wills, and trusts. He learned the laws governing his state's estate taxes and probate, which he was determined to avoid paying.

He knew the threshold in his state under which no estate taxes would be owed, which at the time was $200,000. (Since then the threshold has gone up to $1 million.) To stay below the threshold, and to "dodge the tax man," Mr. Quinn put cash (somewhere between $300,000 and $600,000, court records state) in two safe-deposit boxes, so these funds would be outside of the taxable estate when he and his wife died.

Such cash-hoarding behaviors were common among this generation.

"He made sure we knew about these safe-deposit boxes and where he kept the keys," Charlie said. "He put our names on the access cards to the boxes, and said that after he and my mother died, all four kids should go and fetch the contents of the boxes and split them up four ways."

Mr. Quinn also kept a meticulous account of not only the cash that went into the safe-deposit boxes, but also of his other assets: land, home, bank accounts, insurance policies, stocks, cash, coin collection, etc. He listed them in great detail in a notebook, court records confirmed. He made sure each of the four children knew where the notebook was, and that Mrs. Quinn understood the details, too, in case he died first, which he did.

When his wife took over the household accounting, court documents reflect, her record keeping was inconsistent and far less detailed.

Just put me on the account

Like the bookkeeping records, Mrs. Quinn's condition went downhill quickly after her husband's death. Her oldest daughter stepped up to care for her. The daughter, one of the two siblings named as executors on the will, also got signing privileges and access to all of her parents' accounts so she could "take care of the bills." She now had complete legal claim and access to all the assets, Charlie said.

"We all appreciated what my sister volunteered to do and trusted her to divide up the assets into four equal shares, according to our parent's wishes," Charlie said. "We were fools."

After their mom died later that same year, the sister emptied the bank accounts, cashed out all the stock, and cleared out the safe-deposit boxes, which at least one other sibling had previously seen "stuffed with one-hundred-dollar bills."

"By the time the rest of us realized what had happened, it was too late," Charlie said.

For the sister's part, she claimed that she'd found the safe-deposit boxes empty, and that their mom had changed her mind after Dad died and wanted everything to go to her.

Anthony Palma, a seasoned wills, trusts, and estates attorney based in Orlando, Florida, knows the story all too well, and quickly pointed out the potholes:

Problem No. 1: When your money is in cash outside of your estate with no protection—as in stuffed in a mattress, in a plastic bag in the freezer, under a stair tread, or in a safe-deposit box to which multiple people have access—it is unlikely to wind up going where you want it to go. "The first person who gets to it will bury it in a hole in the backyard and claim they never saw it, or that the safe-deposit box was empty, and you're done," Palma said.

Solution: The best way to protect assets in a safe-deposit box is to just put your name on it. After you die, your beneficiaries will need a court order to open it, and when they do, the bank has to do an accounting of the inventory. If you put two or more names on the account, anyone listed can access the box on his or her own.

More important, don't try to fool the system. Don't hide assets, especially cash, which leaves no trace if someone makes off with it. (See the box below for better, more legal ways to avoid taxes.)

Identify all large assets, including the contents of a safe-deposit box, and put them in a trust with a **title** and a beneficiary. To legitimately protect assets and find airtight ways to distribute them, work with a professional estate planner or lawyer.

Problem No. 2: Take care when choosing executors. When one child in a family has access to all the accounts, the opportunity for "undue enrichment"—let's call it stealing—is great, and the family has few protections. A common tack is for an adult child to take a parent aside and ask to be put on the account so the adult child can help pay the bills. But once the last parent dies, even if the parents had set up proper estate docs, that money's as good as gone, Palma said.

Solution: To avoid that scenario and to block the family interloper, as soon as a parent shows signs that he or she is incapable of managing the finances, the other children need to act fast. When a parent becomes unable to make decisions, undue influence can enter, and family members should swoop in while the person is alive and get a guardian of the court appointed. If the bad actor has already moved funds, the guardian can report back to the judge that the parent does not have capacity to authorize these transfers and ask that the transfers get reversed.

> *"What could and should have been a great and fair passing of one generation's resources to the next generation became instead a tragedy that tore our family apart, dishonored our parents' wishes, and made a bunch of lawyers rich."*
> **—Charlie Quinn**

Sadly, the Quinn siblings spent the next ten years lawyered up and fighting in court. The case finally ended after two appeals, but not to anyone's liking. The older sister did have to restore some of the money. But in the end, two thirds of the assets went to the lawyers.

"Don't assume that if you decide to use family members to execute your wishes, it will go as you planned," said Quinn, reflecting on his experience. "Despite my parents' thorough planning, my siblings and I did not foresee that a trusted daughter and sister would betray her family by abusing her access.

"What could and should have been a great and fair passing of one generation's resources to the next generation became instead a tragedy that tore our family apart, dishonored our parents' wishes, and made a bunch of lawyers rich."

Lessons Learned the Hard Way

While Charlie Quinn can't change what his parents did, he can certainly make sure it does not happen again in his family. Here's what he's learned.

- **Keep it legal.** Get legal help to make sure all paperwork is written, witnessed, and properly filed. This includes wills, appointment of executors, powers of attorney, trusts, homesteads, safe-deposit boxes, bank account access, do-not-resuscitate orders, and beneficiaries on insurance policies and other investments. Be sure everyone you name in the paperwork is willing to perform and aware of their duties, and that they have the contact information they will need. As retired trusts and estates attorney Howard Zaritsky of Rapidan, Virginia, said when I shared this situation with him, "While situations like this aren't unusual, parents who do this are technically asking their family to commit tax fraud. We have better, legal ways to avoid paying taxes." (See the box below.)

- **Pick the right executor.** Most people appoint a family member for this role. That said, Palma noted, "I am constantly filing petitions to remove people who were placed in positions of trust who shouldn't have been." Consider setting up accounts so no one individual can take it all. Or, if no one is trustworthy, hire a corporate trustee adviser. "When large sums of money are at stake, even loving, kind family members can change. Once you give full access to a so-called trusted person (for example, putting the person on all of your bank accounts), those assets legally transition to that person after you die and are no longer in your estate. That person can simply keep everything, and it can be difficult to get back, if not impossible."

- **Share sooner rather than later.** Older parents should give to their adult children or to charities as much as is comfortable for them while they are alive and enjoy the pleasure of seeing their gifts help others, Quinn said. Most children need more financial help early on, when they are in college, buying and furnishing a home, and raising children, as compared to later. Getting the cash when they're in their seventies may not have the positive impact you'd hoped for. Dying with a small amount left in your estate because you have already given away your assets is a strategy worth considering. You leave a lot less behind to fight over. One estate lawyer told me of a client who says, "I'd rather give with a warm hand than a cold one."

- **Consider sharing beyond your family.** Name worthwhile organizations to benefit from your estate when you die.

Better Ways to Avoid Taxes (Than the Freezer)

In this world nothing can be said to be certain, except death and taxes.
—Benjamin Franklin, founding father of the United States
(1706–1790)

Ben Franklin, of course, is right. Going to great lengths to avoid death or taxes is a proverbial waste of time. Extreme tax-avoidance may strike some as simply un-American. At some point, we all have to pay our dues.

That said, just as you can reduce your income tax through deductions, exemptions, and credits, you can use similar legal vehicles to reduce estate taxes, said Palma. Right off the bat, every individual has an exemption credit of $11.58 million that they can pass on to beneficiaries without paying any estate tax. So unless you will be leaving more than that, this is a moot issue.

A marital deduction lets you leave your estate, regardless of its size, to your spouse tax-free. A financial adviser can also help arrange a generation-skipping trust that could further reduce or eliminate estate taxes. In this case, you move assets out of your estate into a trust for your grandchildren. Because the asset skips over your children, they are not responsible for potential tax liability, either.

Two other kinds of trusts—**charitable remainder trusts** and **charitable lead trusts**—can also help provide children with income without tripping a big tax bill. With a remainder trust, the donor gives a large amount to a charity, which then pays the donor or the heirs a steady amount over a period of years, or until the donor or last beneficiary dies. Then the remainder goes to the charity. A charitable lead trust does the reverse. The charity gets the money first and receives a revenue stream over a period of years, then the remainder goes to the heirs. This works well if the adult children don't need the funds right away and can wait several years.

Having assets in a trust adds even greater protections, including the four most people want: divorce protection, creditor protection, bloodline protection, and estate tax avoidance for generations. Putting cash in the freezer or under a stair tread doesn't do any of that. It's simply bad planning.

Part Three

PAINT YOUR CANVAS

I can always choose, but I must know that if I do not choose, that is still a choice.

—JEAN-PAUL SARTRE, French philosopher (1905–1980)

Wills are for rich people. I have plenty of time. I don't have enough assets to leave anyone. It's too expensive. I don't want to think about this now. I don't know where to begin. Before I started writing this book, I'd had all of these thoughts at one time or another. Each time I was wrong. I came to this subject like many, naïve and in denial. The chapters ahead will set you straight, provide you with the tools, and show you the way. If I can do this, you can, too. And trust me, you should.

CHAPTER 11

Put It in Writing

Demystifying wills and trusts

When clients come in to see estate lawyer Anthony Palma of Orlando, Florida, he gets personal right away.

"Show me what you own and what you owe" is how he starts a meeting with clients who want to create an estate plan. He then asks them to produce any current estate documents to make sure they won't hinder, undermine, or conflict with any new plan components. (See the appendix for a checklist on what to bring to your first meeting with an adviser.)

With those basics in hand, his next question is: "What do you want to do?"

And that's your moment.

Not to blow this out of proportion, but this is your chance to change your fate, leave your mark, better the world, alter eternity.

The problem, Palma said, is many people don't step up. "They rely on attorneys to just fill in the blanks and forget to make this plan theirs."

And that is sad.

"Your estate plan is your canvas," he said. "It's yours to paint. Just make sure you do it. Your job is to tell me what you want. My job is to see that you get it."

So take time to reflect, then put it in writing.

Like every other tax, legal, and financial professional I talked to, Palma said more than 95 percent of his clients opt to leave all their money to their family—their spouse or partner, their kids, or their grandkids, in that order. The ones who leave money to charity are either extremely wealthy or never had children (a combination, I've mentioned only half facetiously, that often goes together).

Regardless of how you want the chips to fall when you're gone, one thing is for sure—they won't go where you want them to unless you plan.

Legal minds have written weighty tomes on the subjects of wills, estates, and trusts, and judges have analyzed and parsed the most obscure aspects of these thorny matters in court and through legal opinions. That means we don't have to.

Instead, as we explore how to leave the legacy you want, we'll take the ten-thousand-foot view, not the in-the-weeds-with-a-microscope view that lawyers, judges, and accountants

> *Not to blow this out of proportion, but this is your chance to change your fate, leave your mark, better the world, alter eternity.*

use in their, with all due respect, bill-by-the-hour environments. What you need to know as you consider how you want your legacy to unfold, what you want to leave to whom, and how to make sure the chips fall just the way you want are what tools you can use, and when.

Once you lay out your goals and wishes, then a trusts and estates lawyer can work to figure out which estate planning tools best fit your situation. Sometimes a simple will is all you need to provide sufficient protection of your property, make sure assets get distributed appropriately, and fulfill your legacy with justice.

Often, if your estate is not large, depending on your age and the state you live in, a will is usually sufficient protection. Even though that means the public can see the value of those assets, and that some assets will go through probate, or that some money might go to pay state estate and inheritance tax, the cost of setting up a will, even including those fees, could be far less than the cost to set up a trust, which can be several thousand dollars.

However, if the estate is large and the assets sizable, or if the family is blended or the dynamics are complicated in other ways, a trust will offer privacy and protection.

Let's look at each tool more closely, then weigh the pros and cons of each.

Wills are not just for rich people

While just about every adult can benefit from having a will or trust, only one in three Americans over the age of eighteen actually has one, according to the 2020 Estate Planning and Wills Study by Caring.com.* More concerning is that the number of adults who have a will has gone down from 42 percent in 2017 to 32 percent in 2020.

Predictably, older adults are more likely to have a will than younger ones, but still, only about half of those over age fifty-five have a will or at least some estate planning document. So that leaves half of all older Americans at risk of dying with no say on where their assets will go.

The two most common reasons for not having a will, according to those surveyed, were "I haven't gotten around to it" and "I don't have enough assets to leave anyone." However, about one in every fifteen respondents said, "It's too expensive to set up" or "I don't know how to get a will or living trust."

You may say you won't care once you're gone, but a will makes life a lot easier for those left behind. How you leave this planet, not just what you leave, is your legacy. Be thoughtful.

Also, forget the notion that wills are for rich people.

"Many believe having a will or trust is only for the very wealthy, but having a will could benefit a lot more people of modest means," said retired trusts and estates lawyer Howard Zaritsky.

---

*caring.com/caregivers/estate-planning/wills-survey

As you'll see in the next section, while hiring a lawyer to help draft your will is probably a good idea, you don't have to hire one. You can write your own will using an online form.

If your situation is fairly clean and straightforward, you likely don't need more than a will. For instance, if you're a single elderly person with not many assets, or the assets are mainly in a brokerage account like Schwab, and your kids are not part of a blended family situation, a will should cover you. Also, if you don't own much property, and what you do own is owned jointly with your spouse or partner and will transfer to that person when you die, a will is, again, probably enough protection.

"If the kids all want the money outright, and they don't care that creditors or spouses can access the money, you don't need a trust," Zaritsky said. "However, if your kids are successful, getting money in a trust is better than getting it outright." With a trust you can create a fund that creditors and spouses in divorce can't reach.

However, if giving the money or assets outright is not possible, having assets in a trust is much better, as that will let you dictate who gets what when, and under what circumstances. Trusts also offer families financial privacy, and can protect assets from probate and taxes, which we'll discuss further in the next chapter.

Although trusts provide a bit more protection, a lot can be done in a will to avoid probate and taxes. Let's take a look at the protections each provides.

Will as protection

A last will and testament is a document prepared by you or an attorney on your behalf that identifies who will be in charge of wrapping up your estate, how your assets will be disbursed and to whom, and, if you have minor children or pets, who will take care of them.

Wills come in several forms, some better than others, and some, well, worthless.

Oral or spoken wills: More than anything else, a will underscores the saying "talk is cheap." Simply saying what you want to happen is probably worthless. Spoken intentions that aren't also in writing are rarely upheld. What's in writing, and ideally validated by an attorney, witnessed and notarized, is what counts. Put it in writing.

Handwritten wills: In about half of the United States, a holographic, or handwritten and signed, will is considered valid. Check with an attorney where you live to see if your state is one of them, and whether you need to do anything more, such as having the document notarized or witnessed, to make a handwritten will valid in your state.

Online wills: Free fill-in-the-blank wills specific to your state are available at the click of a mouse on sites like eForms (eforms. com). These online wills are a good starting point, as they get you thinking about what to address. The site will tell you what else your state requires, but you'll still want an attorney to review the document in light of your circumstances to make sure it covers the bases, to flag and fix weak spots, and to eliminate grounds for a challenge.

For a small fee (currently $89 for a Basic Last Will and $279 for a Basic Living Trust), you can also use a LegalZoom (legalzoom.com) document. Either online option is better than not having a will at all. Just be sure you print it out and sign it. A filled-out unsigned electronic form stored on your computer is generally not considered valid. Again, because some states are more lenient, if your parent dies and the only will you have is unsigned on their computer, check with an attorney to see if it's enforceable.

Simply, I love you: The simplest wills are sometimes called "I Love You" wills. When a married couple own everything jointly, their wills simply say that the surviving spouse gets everything. The expectation, of course, is that the surviving spouse and the one who died agreed on what they wanted for their children, other family members, and the charities they supported.

However, most wills are not that simple. Today, as I mentioned earlier, at least 40 percent of families live in some form of divorced or stepfamily relationship, where one or both partners have children from a prior marriage. In two of every five marriages one partner has been married before, and in one in every five marriages (my hand is up) both have.

Full siblings, half-siblings, stepsiblings, children born outside a marriage, ex-husbands, third wives, and so on complicate matters exponentially, creating an array of legal dynamics, and the stuff of family drama—or trauma. Many of the ugliest lawsuits come about when family members try to enforce or defeat wills in the context of a blended family.

But thanks to this book, that's not going to happen to you, right? Working with an estate attorney now, as DC and I did, can help ensure that your assets don't go to the kids of your ex-husband's new wife later.

Bombproof Your Will

Though every will has the potential to be challenged, here are four steps you can take that experts say will help make sure your will holds up under fire.

- **Speak up.** Ask, don't assume, that the person you've named to be executor of your will or the guardian of your children is willing. Talk to them about the responsibility, what that involves, and, in the case of children, how you will help provide for them (perhaps through a life-insurance policy). Also talk to your kids about how assets will be divided and distributed. Eliminate surprises.

- **Keep it current.** Change your will as your circumstances change. (See the box on "When to Revisit Your Plan" at the end of this chapter.) For example, say you sold the Corvette that in your will you promised to Cousin Bobby, and in its place you bought a Ford. Now what? Or maybe since you wrote your last will you bought a diamond necklace you want to leave to your sister. If that's not in your will, someone else might get it. Or maybe that black sheep nephew you had disinherited has redeemed himself and you now want to leave him some money. These changes can all be made by a **codicil**, a fancy word that simply means a change to the will.

- **Be clear.** If you want to leave money to an organization or entity, clearly identify it. Don't simply say "my school." Lack of specificity or getting the name wrong could cause your money to go to your children's school rather than to your university as you intended.

- **Have it notarized.** A notary is a publicly appointed official who can legally verify that the person signing a document is truly that person, to verify a will is not forged. Thus, having your will notarized—that is, taken to a notary who will verify that you signed it—is an important step in making a will official. You might pay a small fee—usually no more than twenty dollars—for this service. Look online for a notary nearby: You can often find them in banks, real estate offices, accounting or law firms, and shipping centers. Mobile notaries are also available to come to you. If you draft your will with an attorney, the attorney's office will likely have a notary available.

The best wills leave no questions. To avoid confusion, discrepancies, infighting, or lawsuits, have an attorney draft your will. Sign it, have it witnessed and validated, and keep it where your loved ones can find it.

So, what if I don't have a will?

Obviously, the main alternative to a will is no will. Despite their many benefits—including the peace of mind and clarity wills provide, the fights they prevent, the legacy they ensure—about half of Americans die without one. In legal terms, not having a will is called dying intestate. Although wills don't have to be complicated or expensive to draw up, many people avoid the task. They procrastinate or don't believe their assets justify the effort. Single folks with no children may believe there's no point, when actually they have as much or more reason. Some don't believe they're old enough to worry about dying, or they are just too busy living to get around to it. Some don't know where to begin.

But all should.

A person who dies intestate has, in essence, made a choice to let the government decide how to distribute his or her assets.

All states have laws called intestacy statutes, which govern how the assets of those who die intestate will get distributed. Most are cookie-cutter approaches that address so-called typical situations, which describes almost no one.

So, not having a will basically means that your state legislature has written your will for you. You lose the opportunity to direct how and to whom your assets should pass when you die. The person the court appoints might not be who you want in control of winding down your affairs.

If you were married and your only children were the biological or adopted children of that marriage, the entire estate would probably be handled fairly. However, as we've said, most families are not "typical." In most states, unmarried couples and stepchildren are not protected by state intestacy statutes. In those cases, these partners and children, although important to you, could be left out.

Those who have no heirs—and who simply let their assets, however small, go where the government chooses—miss out on the chance to benefit a cause they truly cared about, such as their church, school, research effort, or animal shelter.

Sometimes, reason prevails, and involved parties may soften the rules.

When my husband's mother died a few years ago, DC learned that her will, which had been written in Pennsylvania, had not been properly signed per Pennsylvania law. So, she technically died intestate. Under Pennsylvania's intestacy laws, that meant none of her grandchildren or the charities she supported would receive anything. To correct this, DC and his sister (the only other child) agreed to honor the wishes she'd expressed in her invalid will, because it's what she would have wanted. Fortunately, no one was in a position to contest.

If yours is not a nuclear family, an attorney can tell you what would happen to your assets if you died without a will. The answer might prompt you to draft one.

"Having a plan is definitely better than having nothing," said Mark Yegsigian, a certified public accountant and financial planner from Laguna Hills, California. "Any agreement you come to is going to be better than what the state decides."

Certainly, designating how you want your legacy to unfold will be better than leaving it all to chance, and leaving a string of disappointed survivors in your wake.

Prince: Music Legend's Life Ends in Discord

The music icon Prince offers a now infamous example of how bad a situation can become when a person dies without a will. When Prince died in 2016, he was unmarried. He had been married twice, but both marriages ended in divorce. He had one child who died young. His parents also predeceased him. His living heirs were ultimately six full or half siblings, who are still fighting for their part of the estate in court. Not only did Prince have substantial assets (and a hefty estate tax obligation), he also left a trove of unreleased music. At this writing, the case is still being hammered out in court. Whatever the result, it likely will not be what the music legend would have wanted. Unfortunately, we'll never know because he didn't put his wishes in writing.

But for His Simple Will . . .

One day in April of 2020, the gavel came down at Caza Sikes, an art appraisal and auction house in Cincinnati. That day, $40,000, the net proceeds from the auction for the estate of Gerald Dan French, a local patron of the arts, went to benefit the Salvation Army and the Shriners Hospital for Children in Cincinnati, the two charities the childless donor had named in his will. Caza Sikes auctioned off the gentleman's art and collectibles, including silver, bronze statuary, and works of art, said auction co-owner Graydon Sikes.

And that was just part of French's legacy.

In the simple two-page will he drafted with estate lawyer Bruce Favret, French stated he wanted everything he owned sold and divided between these two charities when he died. The value of his total estate, including his condo, exceeded $600,000, according to estate attorney Elizabeth Favret, Mr. Favret's daughter, who acted as French's executor.

"If Dan French had not had a will," she said, "this would have been a mess. The court would have had to do an heir search to find his distant relatives, with whom he had no relationships, and they would have gotten all the money. None of it would have gone where he wanted."

Because he had a will, not a trust, his property still had to go through probate, but it was a clean, straightforward process, she said. The will took away all the guesswork.

Trust as armor

Perhaps the best and most underused vehicle to protect assets, preserve wealth, and, if done right, leave our loved ones enriched and our family intact is the trust. A wealth-preserving tool whose roots date back to the Middle Ages, a trust is a legal entity that can own or hold assets apart from an individual. Trusts can legally separate assets (the **corpus**) from the person setting up the trust (the **settlor**). This arrangement offers important layers of protection and privacy, can help families avoid probate and sometimes taxes, and provides even more assurance that your money, property, and possessions go where you want them to, when you want them to. Because documents in a trust do not get filed with the court, nor are they made public upon your death, your finances and estate can remain private. (Again, the exception is the testamentary trust, which is created within a will.)

Although many kinds of trusts exist, every trust has these four elements:

1. **A settlor.** The person who creates and funds the trust.
2. **A trustee.** The person named in the trust who carries out the settlor's wishes.
3. **Beneficiaries.** One or more heirs or organizations that will receive benefits.
4. **A corpus.** The assets in the trust.

Of the various types of trusts, the two most common are revocable and irrevocable. One you can change, and one you can't.

The revocable living trust: Today, the revocable living trust is the most common because of its flexibility. So long as you, the settlor or owner, are alive, you can alter the trust's terms and add or remove assets. The trust is revocable by you so long as you live. When you die, however, the revocable living trust becomes irrevocable, and the trustee you name must comply with the terms of the trust.

Another advantage of the revocable living trust is that, like a will, this trust can be written to say just what you want, and you can easily change the terms if your financial situation or family relationships change. While these trusts may help you avoid probate, the assets may still be subject to taxes.

Married couples can have a revocable living trust together. When the last partner dies, the trust becomes irrevocable.

The irrevocable trust: With an irrevocable trust, whatever assets you put in and arrangements you make, you may not access again or change—*unless* all the beneficiaries agree. So why would anyone do this? Because once you put assets in an irrevocable trust and "gift" it to, say, your toddler to collect when she turns twenty-one, you avoid paying taxes on this "gift" and its growth. This vehicle effectively removes the assets from your estate.

Irrevocable trusts are less common today because they can put families in a difficult spot. Those who opt to create irrevocable trusts typically do so when their estate is large and they want to avoid paying taxes on the growth, but that may not turn out to be such a good idea.

"That may sound good today when Johnny and Susie are doing well," said Yegsigian, "but what if Johnny becomes a drug addict and has all this access to money with no strings attached, and you've prevented yourself from making changes."

Charitable trusts: If you want to use your legacy to help others beyond your family, consider creating a charitable trust, which, as the name implies, must be for a charitable purpose. Today, most charitable trusts are set up as nonprofit corporations or charitable foundations. Charitable remainder trusts, as they are sometimes called, are also irrevocable. Because they reduce the taxable income of those setting them up, once the money goes in, the money may not go back to the settlor's estate. If you want to establish a charitable trust or foundation, a qualified attorney or accountant can help you.

Because each type of trust has different tax implications, you'll want an attorney or certified financial planner to help you choose and set up the one best suited for your situation.

What goes in a trust?

Besides cash in accounts set up in the name of the trust, other assets you can include in your trust are homes you own, rental properties, cars, boats, investment accounts, collectibles, artworks, and jewelry. Any of the items that have a title, like a house or a car, will need to have their titles changed so the trust owns them, not you personally. For instance, if Mr. and Mrs. Jones share the title on their second home in North Carolina and they want that property protected by their trust to avoid probate, they would have to change the property's title so that it's owned by the Jones Family Trust.

Pick the right trustee

Perhaps the hardest part of creating a trust is picking the trustee, said attorney Zaritsky. "Clients should spend more time picking the trustee than drawing up the trust. Trustees often have huge discretion. You don't want a dilettante or an amateur on the job."

A trustee's role is to administer the trust and invest the property with the fund's best interest in mind—in other words, he or she has a fiduciary duty not to squander it. The trustee is also responsible for making distributions. You want someone who is financially savvy and trustworthy.

Although a family member may be suitable for this role, usually they are not the best choice because they have a dog in the fight, he said. "The ideal trustee is a professional who is not personally involved, but who gets paid a fee for managing the fund according to the terms of the trust," Zaritsky said. Though that is optimal, he added, most clients go with a family member.

Tom Thomas, a certified public accountant based in Winter Park, Florida, and a founding partner at Thomas, Zurcher, and White accounting firm, has been helping clients set up their estate plans for more than forty years, and has served as trustee on numerous estates. Rather than pay a trustee a percentage of the estate's assets, he recommends working with a professional who charges an hourly rate. "Clients will almost always come out ahead if they do." He also recommends spelling that stipulation out in your planning documents.

When a bank serves as a trustee, the bank can potentially have a conflict of interest, he points out. Thomas once had a client who wanted to use money from his trust to buy a car and pay for it in cash. "This wasn't a fancy car, like a Lamborghini," he said. "It was along the lines of a Ford Explorer." But the bank trustee would not release the funds, and instead made the beneficiary finance the car through the bank. This way the bank not only got to receive the annual trustee fee (the amount, usually 0.5 to 1 percent of the total assets, the bank gets each year for managing the trust), but also got the interest on a no-risk loan.

If a professional trustee is performing poorly, sometimes beneficiaries can get together and have the person removed for nonpersonal reasons, said Zaritsky. For example, let's say the trustee is a bank, and the bank gets acquired by a larger bank, and the beneficiaries don't want a larger bank handling the trust's affairs; they could change trustees. But if the beneficiaries didn't have a good reason to change, if their reason was simply that the bank wouldn't do what they wanted, "Good luck finding a bank who will take them on."

Who should have a trust?

While a will is almost never a bad idea, trusts aren't for everyone. However, many of the experts I spoke with agreed that far more people could benefit from these protective legal structures than currently do. "You can't draw a line and have everyone fall on one side or the other," said Zaritsky, "but as a general rule, the greater the value of the estate, the greater the need for a trust. The need is also greater when a family is blended."

A person's age is another factor. For example, an eighty-year-old with $300,000 might be a candidate for a trust, while a twenty-five-year-old with no children with that same amount probably wouldn't be, said Palma, because the younger person's financial picture is likely to change more.

Another reason that one may choose to have a living trust is to avoid probate. As discussed in chapter 4, probate is a court-directed legal process that can be long and costly—especially for larger estates.

"In general, the bigger the estate, the more you want to keep it out of probate, so the more likely you'll want to set up a trust," Palma said. "That said, a lot of clients say, 'Just give me a simple will. I'm not spending the money to set up a trust.'"

Though no minimum amount of money or assets are required to set up a trust, because they can cost several thousand dollars in legal fees to create, you want to have enough to make the effort worthwhile.

"The nice thing about a trust is they allow you to be really detailed," said Yegsigian. "If you're going to keep the family on good terms after you're gone, remove all the obstacles that could create friction and provide detailed instructions, so what you want gets dictated from the grave. Boom. Boom. Boom. No discussion. The kids can then say to each other, 'If you don't like what Mom and Dad wanted for you, take it up with them in heaven.'"

Wills versus Trusts

To recap, here's a summary comparison of wills and trusts.

Wills

- State who's in charge after you die, and how you want your assets distributed.

- Provide for heirs to receive their money outright.

- Do not prevent certain assets, such as property in your name only, from going through probate or being taxable. See the next chapter for a list of assets that avoid probate.

- Are less expensive to create. Costs range from free (if you prepare yours online) to several hundred dollars to potentially a few thousand dollars.

- Are filed with the county court in the county where the deceased person lived, so information is publicly available.

- Are generally for those with more modest assets and simple nuclear families, or both.

Trusts

- State that you don't own your assets, the trust does, and also state who's in charge of distributing those assets.

Designate who will receive the money (the beneficiaries), when and under what conditions.

- Offer protection from probate, taxes, creditors, and in-laws.

- Can cost $3,000 to $10,000 to create, and more for large, complicated estates.

- Are not filed with the court, so financial arrangements and asset values remain private.

- Are generally for those who have significant assets, blended families, or both.

When to Revisit Your Plan

Once you've created your estate plan—and congratulations, by the way!—don't forget about it. Give your plan a once-over every three to five years, *or* when you have a significant life event such as the following:

- A new child or grandchild

- A child or grandchild turns eighteen

- A child or grandchild needs educational funding

- Anyone named in your will—the guardian for your children or your executor—has had a change in their circumstances that makes fulfilling their role difficult or impossible

- A change in marital status

- Another dependent

- A death in the family

- A significant change in financial status

- The addition of a large asset, like a home

- A large increase or decrease in the value of assets, such as investments or loans and debts

CHAPTER 12

Build Your Fences

Keeping out the taxman, creditors,
in-laws, and other interlopers

E ven after forward-thinking folks create a will or a trust, sometimes the best-intended plans go awry. That handwritten will taped under the kitchen table doesn't hold up. The wrong executor or trustee is in charge. A dishonest family member tries to "outsmart" the system. We'll talk about the what-not-to-do list shortly, but first let's look at what more you can do to get the outcome and protection you want.

When clients come to see an attorney about setting up a will or trust, their top concerns are typically avoiding taxes and probate, and protecting their assets from creditors and from going to those outside the bloodline. The way to do that is to create fences, said attorney Anthony Palma.

Tax concerns

Realistically, however, most people don't have to worry about paying the estate or gift tax because the limits are so high. Under today's guidelines, each spouse can leave up to $11.58 million to their beneficiaries, or over $22 million total for a married couple, without having heirs owe any federal estate tax. Because these numbers can change, even dropping to half that in just a few years, be sure to consult your accountant or estate attorney about how your state handles estate taxes.

"If that threshold drops, having a trust won't just be a good idea; for many it will be necessary," Yegsigian said.

Under today's limits, if a parent leaves you an amount greater than the $11.58 million threshold, you will pay estate tax only on the amount over that. But those taxes are steep: The federal estate tax was up to 40 percent in 2020.

Although tax-avoidance need not be your number one concern, if it is, one way to avoid paying taxes is to donate more to charity, which is 100 percent tax-free.

During Zaritsky's forty years of practicing estate law, he said, concerns about taxes were what drove most clients in. "But taxes are the easiest part of estate planning," he said. "Although taxes are incredibly complicated, they are number puzzles. You work them out. We have half a dozen moves to minimize tax liability. You then tell your client, 'This is the best I can do,' and they say, 'Fine.'"

When experts point out that charitable contributions can greatly reduce what their estate will owe in taxes, some clients love the idea. Then experts can work with them to set up charitable remainder trusts, which removes the asset from the donor's estate, and creates an income stream back to the donor or his beneficiaries during their lifetime.

Lawyers who work in this area make it their business to know the tax law and work it to apply to their client's situation to offer the maximum benefit. This is also where lawyers get creative.

Palma shared the example of one client he worked with who had a large estate. He abhorred the thought of giving any of the money to the government. As he was getting toward the end of his life, he wanted to set up an estate plan that would ensure that none of his money went to pay taxes after he died. So he bought a $50 million life-insurance policy and paid an $8 million premium for it up front. He named his kids as beneficiaries. Then he transferred ownership of the policy to the kids. (It's key to make sure both that the kids—not the estate—are beneficiaries *and* that the policy ownership gets transferred to the kids.) And then he left everything he owned to charity—a tax-free contribution.

When he died, the kids got the full $50 million and paid no taxes because insurance benefits are not considered income. Thus, he was able to give his children a gift well beyond the $11.58 million tax threshold, without their having to pay taxes. He was also able to leave tax-free money to charity, resulting in a classic win-win for everyone but the government—exactly the result the client wanted.

Life insurance can be set up so it's estate-tax-free, which makes it a great planning tool, said Zaritsky. With good planning, you can get both spouses tax exemptions, and then throw in life insurance.

Again, dealing with the taxes is the easy part. After that's resolved, knottier problems surface.

"The real problems are trying to cope with the family baggage that has been created by a lifetime of slightly off-kilter relationships," Zaritsky said. "The totally harmonious family is not mythical, but it's close to it."

Dealing with the fallout of which parent liked which kid best—that's what generates all the litigation and rips families apart. "That's not something estate attorneys can fix, but we are expected to. These problems build up over decades, and the people who built them up are the last people to be able to fix them."

GOOD TO KNOW

According to the Tax Foundation, the following states plus the District of Columbia have estate taxes: *Connecticut, Hawaii, Illinois, Maine, Maryland, Massachusetts, Minnesota, New York, Oregon, Rhode Island, Vermont, and Washington.*

The following six have inheritance taxes (Maryland is the only state that has both): *Iowa, Kentucky, Maryland, Nebraska, New Jersey, and Pennsylvania.* All states are subject to federal estate tax.

Creditor protection and the four magic words

The next protection those creating an estate plan want is assurance that creditors can't get to the trust's assets, Palma explains. Let's say you leave money in a living trust to your son, who gains access to the funds when he turns twenty-one. At age twenty-five, he gets sued and loses. He then gets deposed. The lawyers sit him down and start asking him what he owns. They ask if he has a trust. He says yes. Next, they start grabbing assets.

"Whether they can get to the assets in the trust all depends on how it's set up," Palma said.

If a trustee manages the trust and disburses the funds to the son, it's creditor protected. That's because when the beneficiary does not have direct access to the funds and a trustee disburses the money, creditors who have claims against the beneficiary can't get to the funds, since they technically belong to the trust.

Now, if the son is the trustee and thus handles his own trust fund, and if the trust doesn't specify what the son must use the funds for, he may be out of luck. However, if the son is the trustee of his own trust and the trust specifies that the funds can only be used for his "health, education, maintenance, and support," it's creditor protected. "Those four magic words— 'health, education, maintenance, and support'—carry immense protection with regard to keeping creditors out," Palma said.

Although estate laws are pretty universal throughout the United States and Canada, check with an estate attorney where you live about the laws in your state.

Keeping it in the family

When creating their estate plan, most people also want assurance that their funds will stay in the bloodline. That is, they want the assets to flow from them to their children and then to their grandchildren, and not to their children's spouses in the case of divorce. My parents' simple will, for instance, is a good example. It was set up so that when the last one of them died, the remaining assets would be divided fifty-fifty between my brother, Craig, who was married with no children, and me, married with two children.

If Craig had died before our last surviving parent, 100 percent of the funds would have gone to me, not to his wife. If I had died before our last surviving parent, my half of the inheritance would not have gone to my brother, nor would it have gone to my husband. It would have passed down the bloodline and been put in a trust for my two children, my parents' only grandchildren. The assets would have been split fifty-fifty and used solely for their benefit and enrichment.

And this is a simple situation!

As it turned out, our family's situation followed a natural course. My parents died before their children. After their debts and obligations were met, Craig and I each received half of their remaining assets. Here's where plans can go awry. If adult children want to keep their inheritance "in the bloodline," they must be careful not to comingle funds with their spouses.

In my case, I had gotten divorced a few years before my mother, my last surviving parent, died, so having my inheritance money going to an ex-spouse wasn't an issue. However, if I had gotten divorced after receiving my inheritance, the only way to protect my inheritance from becoming a joint asset would have been to not comingle the funds. That can be easier said than done.

"A cardinal rule for married couples is that if one partner inherits money, he or she should not mix those funds with jointly owned assets," said Florida CPA Tom Thomas, also a personal financial specialist who serves as trustee for many clients. Depending on the state, most estate planning attorneys will suggest that the heir place the inherited money in a trust for another layer of protection.

That's what I did. When I remarried, I created a trust with the funds I inherited. My two children are the beneficiaries. I manage the funds, and can use the money for my own purposes. I can borrow from it to, say, buy a car, which I have, and then pay the trust back. I have also used the funds to help my daughters with housing while they are in graduate school. When I die, what remains will fall to them equally, and then to their children, and not to my spouse. DC has a similar setup.

"Heirs have a responsibility to protect their inheritance. Even if a trust protects assets left to adult children, heirs can mess up their parents' intention if they're not careful," Thomas said. "If you inherit a significant amount from your parents and your spouse or partner talks you into using that money to buy a bigger house, for example, the funds used to buy that joint asset become theirs, too."

Here's another scenario: Say a father dies and he leaves an inheritance to his daughter, who is married with children. Then the daughter dies, and her husband remarries. The father's original intention was to make sure his money flowed to his grandchildren, not to his former son-in-law and his new wife and her kids. He could make sure that happened as long as his lawyer put up the right fences.

If you, as an heir, want to keep your money in your bloodline as your parents would have wished, keep the money in a separate account, or a trust. A properly written document, one that has a few "fences" and other precautions, will make sure the money stays with the bloodline and doesn't go to support an unrelated party.

"Once we open clients' eyes to their exposures, they see what can happen and understand," Palma said.

A divorce, of course, is when assets are at greatest risk.

Joke: Why is divorce so expensive?
Answer: Because it's worth it.

Paul McCartney: Money Can't Buy Me Love

You may recall when former Beatle Paul McCartney married Heather Mills in 2002, four years after his wife of twenty-nine years, Linda, died of cancer. Against the advice of experts, McCartney and Mills had no prenuptial agreement. They separated four years later, and their divorce was final in 2008. Mills got $50 million.

How? we all asked. Palma explained: Even though McCartney kept his funds segregated, the judge asked what he was worth when they got married. What was he worth when they split up? He was worth $100 million more, and Mills got half.

"Paul McCartney is a guy who marries forever," Palma said. "He didn't expect this."

He should have had a prenuptial agreement at a minimum, and on top of that a trust, Palma said. "A trust could have kept all that separate. We put fencing up. Never just one, a bunch of fences, so when challengers crash through one, they run into another one. We add layers of protection."

When McCartney married the third time, he got a prenup.

Probate workarounds

Whenever you hear the word "probate," the word "avoid" is never far away. However, Carol Zurcher, also a CPA and partner at the Thomas, Zurcher, and White accounting firm, offers this reassurance: "Probate is not that awful. Often when working through an estate of someone who died, we will find an asset, like a stock certificate, that didn't make it into the trust, and so has to go through probate, and it's no big deal."

That said, trusts are one of the best ways of making sure assets don't have to go through that legal labyrinth. And some assets that are not part of a trust also get to bypass the sticky probate patch. These probate-dodging vehicles are sometimes called **non-probate will substitutes**, which is a mouthful, but just means these assets are not in the will nor in a trust and they don't go through probate. They offer a free ride. What these assets typically have in common is a named beneficiary. Here are the main ones:

Retirement accounts. By far the largest category of assets that don't have to go through probate are retirement accounts. These include defined benefit plans (pensions) and defined contribution plans (401(k)s or 403(b)s, IRAs, and annuities). Generally, the assets in these plans pass to beneficiaries outside of probate, assuming you've filled out the beneficiary form properly.

Bank accounts. If you have a bank account that is payable to another person on death (POD) or transferable on death (TOD), that will not go through probate. Again, be sure you've filled out the beneficiary line correctly, and that if your relationship with the named beneficiary changes, as in the case of divorce or estrangement, you stop to update your beneficiary.

Life insurance. If you have a life-insurance policy that names a beneficiary, the proceeds of that policy will go directly to the named beneficiary or beneficiaries outside of probate.

Investment or brokerage accounts with named beneficiaries.

Trust assets, such as real estate, bank accounts, loans payable to you, and other assets that make up the corpus of the trust.

Assets owned jointly with rights of survivorship—that is, property you own with someone else who assumes your right of ownership if you die. (See chapter 14 for more on how to title assets.)

Assets that *are* usually subject to probate are cash, bank accounts that don't have TOD instructions, retirement accounts and investments that don't name beneficiaries, real estate, and assets held as tenants in common.

GOOD TO KNOW

The person you name in these retirement documents will trump whatever you say in your will, so get your names straight. For instance, if you named your first wife as the beneficiary in your IRA paperwork and said in your will that this retirement asset should go to your second wife, wife number two will be disappointed.

CHAPTER 13

How Much for the Kids?

*Divide assets equally or based
on need or performance?*

———————————

You often see in movies—*Knives Out* comes to mind—a dramatic scene where a family is tensely sitting around while a lawyer reads "the Will." Gasps and fainting follow.

In reality, "that's not done," said attorney Howard Zaritsky, for many reasons. One being that the time to read the will to your family is while everyone is still alive. "You tell them, 'Here's what's going to happen and here's why. You may not like it, but this is what I've decided.' The best surprise is no surprise."

For some, however, getting to that point takes the courage of Rosa Parks and the wisdom of Solomon. Although some matriarchs and patriarchs avoid sharing the plan because they don't want to stir arguments, experts universally agree that the best way to prevent sibling relationships from becoming worse after a parent dies is to leave no surprises.

Evenly divided or need based?

Choosing how much will go to each heir is not always as simple as it would seem. The obvious solution, one that seems fair, is to treat all the kids equally and leave each child the same amount. That can work fine, except when it doesn't.

Zaritsky rolls out a few scenarios:

- What if the daughter is a surgeon who makes tons of money, and her brother teaches guitar? Should she get less? She could argue that her brother's choices are not her fault.

- What if you have two kids who are successful professionals, and a third who has a learning disability and will never make more than minimum wage? Do you divide equally, or give a little more to the one who doesn't have as much? Good luck.

- What if one kid says, "But I stayed in the family business and worked with Dad my whole life while you got to go off to college and have your own career, so I deserve more." And the sibling says, "I don't think so! You got the family business, and I had to go out and make my own way. I deserve more."

"There is no formula for what will and will not upset people," Zaritsky said. Every trusts and estates attorney can tell a story of a family that fell apart after the matriarch or patriarch died.

"Most attorneys see it coming," he said, "but there's not much we can do. Most families are held together by someone with a strong personality and a large purse. While they're alive no one will cross them, but after they die, a lot changes."

Estate lawyers can help head off problems by assessing each family's situation. "This is when the conversation gets even more personal," Palma said. "Clients need to be honest about their kids. Every child is different. What if you have one who is terrible with money, or has a drug issue, or you have a dishonest kid, or a kid who is lazy, or one who dates bums?" Then, when setting up a trust, you might build in incentive provisions, or restrict distributions so they're based on the child meeting clear, distinct standards.

For the loafer, you might build in incentives to work. The more you work, the more you get. The one with a drug issue can't have the money unless he has three clean drug screenings. Good lawyers have ways of helping parents address financial, motivational, drug, or other personal issues and setting up the terms of the trust accordingly. But you have to be forthcoming.

"Get ready to bare your soul. You can't be embarrassed. We are sometime lawyers, sometimes psychiatrists."

Two Brothers: One Spender, One Saver

Years ago, CPA Mark Yegsigian had a client who got an inheritance from his dad of about $3 million. The payments were to be spread out over ten years in three equal payments. The client's brother got the same amount of money, but all up front.

"At first I thought that was shabby," Yegsigian said, "but lo and behold, the dad was spot-on. My client blew through his first payment long before he got the second one, which was spent before he got the third payment. Meanwhile, the other brother had invested the money and more than doubled his funds." Parents know their kids.

Once Palma gets a feel for his clients, their wishes, and their situation, he starts making recommendations. "How about if we do it this way? Have you thought of this?" Then he starts modeling.

Caroline is a friend of mine who lost her husband to cancer in 2018. The couple had three children. Since they knew he was dying, they had the time and motivation to plan. They set up two revocable living trusts, one in his name and one in hers. When he died, she gained control of his trust, which became irrevocable and continues to grow. She does not plan to draw from it in her lifetime. His trust remains separate from her trust, which she does draw from.

When Caroline, now sixty, dies, the trusts will merge, then be divided to form three separate trusts, of equal amounts, one for each child. A corporate trustee from Charles Schwab will manage the distributions. Although the trusts are equal in size, Caroline and her husband, knowing how their kids were with money, agreed on different conditions for how the funds will get distributed.

All three children will gain access to their trusts when they turn thirty-five, or after Caroline dies, which ever happens last. Their son, who has special needs and is bipolar, will receive a monthly distribution "to maintain a reasonable lifestyle" at the trustee's discretion.

The two daughters can either take some or all of the amount when they turn thirty-five, or they, too, can ask for the trustee to pay them a monthly distribution to "maintain a reasonable lifestyle."

So, for example, Caroline explained, if a reasonable lifestyle is an annual income of $75,000, and one of the girls is earning $100,000 a year in her job, she would get the $75,000 lifestyle distribution on top of that.

It's also up to each of the adult children to predetermine where they want the remaining inheritance to go if one of them dies. "They can leave it to their spouse, or to their kids, or to the SPCA, if they choose," Caroline said. If they don't say, it goes to their siblings.

And Caroline has another provision in the trust from her husband. "It's the cabana boy provision," she jokes. If she remarries, her spouse has to disclaim any interest in the trust fund. If he doesn't, she loses the money in that trust.

Another friend of mine set up an irrevocable trust for her two children, who would get their money when they turned thirty. She wanted to move the assets out of her estate by "gifting" it to her children so she could minimize her taxes. She ultimately regretted giving up access to the funds, which she later needed.

So how much is enough to leave each child? As the proverbial guideline goes, "Enough to make them independent but not so much that they don't have to work." Once you figure out how much that is, then you can layer in any conditions you would like each child to meet before they get their funds. Maybe they must first graduate, or if using the money for a down payment on a house, they have to match the money down with their own. The trustee can verify that these conditions are met.

Tom Thomas often advises his clients to offer distributions by matching funds in an "earn-it-out" arrangement. "Rather than give kids the money outright, set up a trust that matches what they earn every year." He's seen cases where kids get large distributions all at once, or, say, every five years, at ages twenty-five, then thirty, then thirty-five. "The inheritance money can undermine the kids' desire to work. When the money runs out, they have wasted their best career-development years and may have a rough time finding employment."

One potential downside of the earn-it-out approach, Zurcher added, is this: "The kids can think, 'There goes Mom again. She tried to control me her whole life, and she's still trying.'"

A lot of that aggravation can be avoided with a conversation.

"The biggest downfall I see is when clients try to control their heirs from the grave," she said. "These clients are either afraid to have the conversation, or they never get around to it while they are alive, and the kids are blindsided by the strings attached to the gift and don't know why. All that confusion could have been prevented if the parent had sat down and explained what they were thinking over a cup of coffee."

A legacy better than money

Beyond money, parents need to realize the best legacy they can leave are kids who can take care of themselves and succeed in the world. Part of that means letting them struggle, Zurcher said. "Parents want to solve every problem, but that doesn't build confidence or teach kids how to take care of themselves."

Denying yourself so you can leave more for your children is not necessarily the best strategy, Zurcher added. If you've been blessed with success, don't shortchange yourself. "Live while you can. Take the trip. Buy the boat. Give your kids tools to do for themselves and be successful. Provide them with a good education, and let them take it from there."

Money is only part of our legacy. The other is to develop good people.

Blended families raise the stakes

Blended families—which, again, include families with single parents, cohabiting couples, and stepfamilies—make up the majority of families in America, and create the most complicated, and most litigated, situations. "They are why lawyers exist," Palma said, only half joking. A good estate planner has to have a couple dozen ideas for how to divide an estate and customize them. Plans are not one-size-fits-all.

Among the greatest challenges is setting up the distribution of assets among "unequal" family members. The solution depends on a number of factors and needs to be evaluated child by child, family by family. But here are some considerations:

- Does the stepchild have another living parent outside your family? If so, what is the child's relationship with this parent? If it's good, that child should have a second source of inheritance. Has the other parent developed an estate plan that includes the stepchild?

- Is the other biological parent estranged, destitute, or dead, in which case you are fulfilling more of a parental role than you might otherwise?

- Is there a concern that the stepchild's living parent will try to access the stepchild's inheritance? If so, you might need to build protections into the trust to prevent that.

- Since what age, and for how long, has the stepchild been part of the blended family? How many months of the year does or did the child live in your home? If the family came together when the child was a toddler, the dynamic is quite different than if the stepfamily formed when the child was in college.

- How do the stepsiblings get along? Do you anticipate any problems among them based on unequal, or even equal, distribution? (Which you are going to explain to them ahead of time, right?)

- What if you are the stepparent and your spouse (the biological parent) dies first? How will you manage the interests of and inheritance of the stepchild?

- Did the stepparent adopt the stepchild?

- Do you want to make a parting statement about unity by treating all children in the blended situation the same? Maybe you equally divide any assets the couple has earned together among their respective children.

As you can see, blended families have much to consider, and a seasoned estate lawyer can offer suggestions about how families with similar dynamics have untangled these thorny issues. The one nonnegotiable factor is that you must have a plan.

Palma tells the tragic story of a couple who got remarried in their fifties. Both had kids from prior marriages. For convenience, they put all their assets in a joint account, then went off to Germany on their honeymoon. They planned to do their life estate planning when they got back. However, while speeding on the autobahn, they got in a car accident. Both died.

Investigators determined that the husband died first. And so, because they owned assets jointly and were married, all his assets went to her as the surviving spouse. When she died moments later, technically everything fell to her kids. When the husband's children said, "You're going to split that, right?" They were unpleasantly surprised by the response.

Palma wasn't. "There are a million cases like that."

The takeaways: Have a plan. Tell the kids. Don't delay.

The best surprise is no surprise

Whatever plan you come up with, don't take it to your grave before others learn about it. Finding out that the division of assets is equal despite the fact that one child stayed home and took care of an ailing parent for a decade, or that the division is unequal because one kid can't support himself and so needs more, are all reasonable ways to divide assets. The problem is, survivors don't like to find out when it's a done deal and they can't discuss it.

Getting any resentment on the table while parents are still around is the key to addressing questions and heading off or smoothing over disagreements, which may, realistically, never be resolved to everyone's satisfaction.

"One of my goals as an estate lawyer was to minimize the number of times a division of an estate broke up a family," Zaritsky said. "Clients don't usually see that as something that can happen. It can and it does."

Your plan may sound perfect to you. You can tell your lawyer, This is how I want to do it. I don't care what my kids think. And if your lawyer is awake, he or she will say: "You do realize they are going to hire lawyers and spend serious amounts of money trying to resolve what they believe are inequities, don't you?"

So, before you decide to take your plan to your grave, think about the trap you are leaving them in. Reviewing your plans with your family while you're alive heads off a lot of ill—pardon the pun—will.

Having a family discussion gives parents a chance to explain to the kids why things are going to be different than they might think. This is also the time to tell their children about the portion of their estate they plan to leave to charity. They can also deliver another reality, that after the taxes get paid and the money gets divided four ways, the children won't have as much as they think, so they should, literally, not bank on it.

"Ideally, having a meeting with your lawyer where you, your spouse, and the primary beneficiaries all attend, and where the plan is presented clearly and questions answered is the best money you can spend," Zaritsky said.

Whether your attorney is present or not, when you deliver the news, be tactful. Don't, for instance, call someone out as a spendthrift, or point out that you think someone's husband or wife is a slouch. Just say matter-of-factly that since Peter is a high school teacher and Mary's a trusts and estates lawyer, we're going to leave a little more to Peter.

After you're gone, the lawyer can take the heat.

But in the end, is it really all about the money? I asked Zaritsky.

"It's never about the money," he said. "The money is just the measure. It's about family relationships. 'I knew Dad liked you better. You got the Porsche.'"

GOOD TO KNOW

After parents die, Zaritsky advises all the kids to sit down and talk things through NOT in front of a lawyer. "Work it out among yourselves. Don't work it out in front of a lawyer. Because if an argument arises, a lawyer has to take action; then you will have two lawyers."

One Father's Legacy: You Reap What You Sow

A good friend of mine who has spent his entire career helping clients manage money told me, when I discussed this book with him, that he believes where you put your money says more about you than almost anything else.

"When you check out and cross that finish line, you are remembered not by how much money you had, but how you used it," he said. Jeff (not his real name because his story gets personal) has been a family friend for decades. We've known each other through prior marriages and pre-kids. As we chatted about estate plans, he shared lots of wisdom and advice, as usual, but perhaps most poignant was his own example.

Jeff, sixty-three, is a divorced dad with two daughters. He is newly engaged to a woman he has been dating for almost ten years. His fiancée is a widow with four sons and three grandkids. Jeff has already named her in his trust and will. She also has her own trust. They are completely separate. If Jeff dies before she does, she will inherit money from Jeff and vice versa. Jeff's daughters will receive their inheritance upon his death as well.

That's where it gets interesting.

At the time we talked, Jeff told me he had just revised his will and trust so that one daughter is set to receive more than her sister. "The year 2020 was the year my daughters crossed over from being treated the same to being treated fairly," he told me. "The respect, love, and compassion one shows her family is quite different from the disrespect and lack of consideration the other shows, so their shares will reflect that.

"One is living a responsible life, working hard on her career and treating other members of the family with kindness," he said. "The other hasn't made such good choices."

Every year, Jeff says, he will reassess and change the amount up or down or leave it alone depending on the circumstances. Making the change is easy. The trust doesn't change. The assets don't change. Just the percentages change. "I send an email to my lawyer saying, 'Please amend the percentages of disbursement in paragraph twelve from this to this,' and we're done."

That's the beauty of a living trust. They can change.

"The day I die my legacy will reflect how I felt about my kids at that time," he said. "Next week, if I get taken out by a car, the message will be 'Too bad you couldn't turn it around.' I don't believe it's fair to treat everyone equally when you're not treated equally. This is your report card today. You have to measure on something."

Treat charity like another child

Of course, leaving everything to your children is not your only option. Maybe they're all wealthy, or all ingrates, or perhaps you can think of a charity that is equally deserving, or more so.

"My belief is that nobody has the right to an inheritance," Zaritsky said. "Spend all your money if you want to. Unless you have a special needs child who cannot take care of him- or herself, that's different. Then you have a moral obligation."

After your family is taken care of—whatever that means to you—consider whether you want to leave any portion of your estate to a cause. You could consider donating a portion to research a particular disease, help the blind, aid veterans, save whales, build schools for girls in lower-income countries. You have zillions of options. Some are worthier than others. (See the section on choosing charities in chapter 9.)

"If I had any advice for those in a position to leave a planned gift, it would be to treat charity like another child," said Brian Fogle, the community foundation leader we met in Part Two. "If you have three children you plan to leave an inheritance to, make charity your fourth."

> *"Kids are less resentful of the money their parents give to charity than of money they give to another kid."*
> —**Howard Zaritsky**

CPA Tom Thomas uses

a different strategy with his own two children. Although he is generous to the causes he supports now, after he's gone, he will count on his kids to pay that forward. "I'd rather leave the money to my kids than to charity and encourage them to be generous and do the right thing. Spend time with your kids and let them know what you would do. Then leave it to them."

No one prescription works for every family, so find the one that works for yours. Whether you lead by example or create a plan that deliberately expresses your intentions, or both, this is your chance to make a difference. And the difference you make could last for generations.

GOOD TO KNOW

Among adults who don't have children, 45 percent leave a planned gift. Among adults who do have children, fewer than 15 percent do. Among those who also have grandchildren, the number of those who leave a planned gift falls to under 10 percent.

—BRIAN FOGLE, president of the Community of
the Ozarks Foundation

Because you likely don't know how many assets you will have the day you cross the finish line, you might want to pledge a percentage rather than a fixed amount. State in your will or trust that you would like 5 or 10 percent of your estate to go to your alma mater.

Although leaving money to charity sounds like a nice idea, very few estate plans have a charitable component, said Palma.

"More than nine out of ten choose to leave all their assets to their kids and grandkids, and rarely to charity. If they leave any to charity, it's not much."

He notes two exceptions. Those with especially large estates, and those who have no children. "You do see clients who have large estates leave a percentage to a foundation and ask that, after their death, their child be put on the board of directors." That gives the deceased donor **le mort main**—literally the dead hand, or influence from the grave.

As the stories in Part Two illustrated, giving to charity has many upsides:

- It feels good.

- It's tax-free.

- It can bring benefit into perpetuity.

And here's one more reason that might motivate you most of all: Charitable gifts create fewer problems than family gifts, Zaritsky has observed. "Kids are less resentful of the money their parents give to charity than of money they give to another kid."

Howard's Plan: What About You?

After a lengthy conversation with Howard Zaritsky in which we talked about several of his cases and clients he'd handled during his nearly forty years of practicing estate law, I turned the tables and asked Zaritsky about his estate plan. Instantly, his voice changed from jaundiced lawyer to impassioned philanthropist.

Zaritsky and his wife, Martha, also a retired trusts and estates lawyer, have been married for forty-seven years and have no children. "Because we don't have kids, the answer was easy. We will leave our assets to causes that matter to us."

He lit up as he told me about the Montpelier Foundation, an organization that teaches visitors about the US Constitution. Located in Orange County, Virginia, where he and his wife also live, the foundation's headquarters is the former residence of James Madison, our nation's fourth president.

"The foundation invites groups like high school civics teachers and police officers to come learn about the Constitution," he said. "I find that very meaningful. It's a wonderful operation."

Besides a sum he and his wife have set aside in their estate to benefit the Montpelier Foundation, they are leaving their home, a mid-nineteenth-century house, to the organization as well.

The foundation will make sure the scenic and conservation easements of their home's property aren't violated so the land cannot be developed and the house will be preserved. When the foundation does sell the property, all proceeds will flow to the organization.

"We live in the country, and big houses in the country don't sell quickly," Zaritsky said. "It could take four to five years. Whether the foundation wants to be patient and wait for that ideal buyer or drop the price for a fast sale is entirely up to them."

Not least, Emory University will also inherit a piece of the couple's legacy. "The school has a meaningful place in our lives and is a major charity for us," he said. "It's where we met."

CHAPTER 14

What Else Can Go Wrong?

Titles trump wills and trusts

No matter how well-written your will is or how solid your trust, one simple fact can pull the rug out from under it all. How an asset—such as a piece of real estate, a bank account, a car, or a portfolio of stocks or bonds—is titled. How a person or a couple or a group of partners hold title to an asset is critical because when an owner dies, any title arrangement will override whatever is stated in a will or trust.

"That's where everyone falls on their face," attorney Anthony Palma said. "The key to creating an estate plan that no one can violate starts with how you title the assets."

Roots in Feudalism

Until now, I'm betting you thought titles were for books, and tenants were renters. To better understand how these terms wormed their way into our discussion of trusts and estates, we need to go back into the mists of the Middle Ages, when between the ninth and fourteenth centuries in France and England feudalism was the dominant social system. This is where our concept of landlord and tenant begins.

Under the feudal system, the king owned all the land. After parceling off what he wanted to live on and setting some aside for religious orders, the king allowed barons to control all the rest in exchange for rent and for soldiers and knights to fight for him.

The barons then could live on part of the land and lease the rest to knights, who paid the barons rent and provided soldiers in exchange. The knights could occupy as much of the land as they liked and let the serfs live on the rest. For the right to live on the land, serfs provided the knights with free labor, food, and services.

So, the king, barons, and knights were the lords of the land, hence "landlords." However, only the king owned the land, or held *title* (from Latin *titulus*, meaning "caption," "inscription," "to put name to") to the land.

"Hold" is the key word, as the word "tenant" comes from the French verb *tenir*, "to hold." Barons, knights, and serfs were *tenants* in that they "held" an estate of another.

This system was in effect until the mid-1300s, when the Black Death, which killed a third of the population of western Europe, decimated the workforce, empowering those who remained. The feudal system began to fail because the remaining serfs were in a position to demand more freedoms and rights to own land, or to leave to find better opportunities.

Today we use the word "title" to describe the document that says we own a piece of property, and the word "tenant" to describe the way we hold that property, which can mean owned or rented.

Here's what can go wrong. Say you and your buddy John own an apartment complex together as joint tenants with rights of survivorship, and your will says that when you die, everything you own goes to your wife. If you die, John gets your share of the apartment complex, not your wife.

That's because *titles trump wills and trusts.* So pay attention to how your assets are titled and make sure they are consistent with your plan.

Whenever someone else shares the title on an asset with you, how you take that title will have a significant bearing on what happens when you die. In other words, how you title an asset has everything to do with whether it lands in the corner pocket you'd aimed for or ricochets and lands in a side pocket (or an ex-spouse's pocket), which wasn't at all what you had planned.

An ironclad estate plan depends on identifying what you own, how it is titled, where it is set up to go when you go, and what contingencies exist that could send it in another direction. Then you have to offset those contingencies.

Types of title

Knowing the different ways you can take title of an asset is important. The three most common are joint tenants with rights of survivorship, tenants by the entireties, and tenants in common. Only the first two allow the surviving owner or owners to avoid probate. Here's how they differ.

Joint Tenants with Rights of Survivorship: This form of joint tenancy can exist between two or more people, and couples don't have to be married. For instance, joint tenants can be a mother and son, siblings, or two or more otherwise unrelated business partners. Assets commonly titled "joint tenants with rights of survivorship" include real estate, bank or brokerage accounts, stocks, and bonds.

Here's how it works: While alive, each partner (or tenant) has full rights of ownership to the portion of the property that he or she contributed—no more. No partner can sell his or her piece of the property without the permission of the other partners. However—and here's the risky part—each owner has full access to all of the property and can withdraw all the funds even though he or she technically owns only a portion.

When one owner dies, that person's share automatically passes to the surviving partner or partners (tenants) and is not subject to probate. However, when the last surviving tenant dies—unless that person adds someone else to the title—the property will go through probate before it goes to any beneficiaries.

Here's what can go wrong: Because what the title says overrides a will and a trust, if your will says you want your ownership in a piece of property to go to your sister, but you hold title to that asset in joint tenancy with your business partner, Jamal, your piece of the property will go to Jamal.

In another example, let's say a husband states in his will that he wants to leave all his property—which consists of his house and his bank account—to his wife when he dies. However, he owns his house in joint tenancy with his sister, and his bank account in joint tenancy with his son. When he dies, his wife gets neither.

Tenancy by the Entireties: Tenancy by the entireties is a form of joint tenancy that can exist only between a married couple. This arrangement was created to protect spouses who had acquired real estate during their marriage, and to prevent one spouse from selling the real estate without the other's permission.

In tenancy by the entireties, each spouse owns an equal share of the asset. Tenancy by the entireties can be dissolved by divorce, death, or sale of the asset. So let's say Bob and Sue are married and own a house together under this title arrangement. Bob dies. His ownership of the house then passes automatically to Sue without going through probate. Sue now owns 100 percent. Again, if you use tenancy by the entireties, make sure that what the title says fits your overall intentions as outlined in your will or trust.

Tenancy in Common: A tenancy in common is the probate exception. When one owner dies, his or her share of the property does not automatically pass to the other tenant in common, and it does not necessarily avoid probate. Rather, it passes per the instructions in the deceased owner's will or living trust. If there is no will or trust, it goes to the individual's heirs. The other owner retains his or her share of the property.

No, you will not be tested on this. I just lay all this out here to show you that the relationships between titles and trusts or wills are complicated. This is yet another reason to work with a lawyer who specializes in this area of law.

The case of the condo

A couple years ago, DC and I bought a condo in Nashville for our youngest daughter to live in while she went to graduate school. We paid for the condo in cash. We each put in a matching amount from our respective trusts. We took title to the property in our names as tenants in common. (You'll recall from our chapter on trusts that your trust is not you. That is, it is a separate entity.)

When our estate lawyer reviewed the deed to the condo, he advised us to retitle and rerecord the deed to show that our trusts, not us individually, each owned a half interest in the property. That way if either of us died before the condo was sold, the assets would stay protected from probate within our respective trusts. If we didn't change the title and one of us died, when the property did sell, the assets of the partner who died would not have received the benefit of the trust, and that person's share would have been subject to probate.

A trust works only if you title the assets so that your trust owns it while you're alive.

To see how your property is titled, look online for the agency that handles deeds in the county where the property is located. If you own a property in your name and you want the trust to own it, you will likely have to file a **quitclaim** deed, which ends your right or claim and transfers ownership to the trust. The legal form allows you to name the person or trust who will assume ownership or "take title" of the property and show the world who owns it. Although laws vary depending on the state, you may be able to access forms online and do this process yourself, or an attorney can help you.

The big point: *If you're going to go to the expense of creating a trust, make sure to "properly fund it"—that is, to move all your assets into it while you're alive. Though this takes a bit of additional effort (such as, in the case of real estate, changing the title and the deed of your property), if your goal is to avoid probate or undesirable comingling of funds, do it.*

CHAPTER 15

Heading Off the Buttinskies

When someone challenges the will

L egal textbooks are full of cases where family members, dissatisfied with their lot, challenged wills in court. They may claim the person who left the will was under undue influence or duress, or they may claim fraud, or that the property suspiciously went to an unlikely person. Some challenges succeed. Some don't. But almost every time a large portion of the estate goes to pay lawyers and court costs.

Often the challenger alleges that another family member or interloper butted in and persuaded the **testator** to change the will. "When dealing with assets like bank accounts, safe-deposit boxes, and real estate, you have to watch out for someone grabbing a parent and seeing a lawyer and being put on the account," Palma said. "It happens all the time" (as you saw in the case of the Quinn family in chapter 10).

Stories about the well-meaning neighbor or nurse are commonplace. They talk to the elderly parent and say, "Your kids never show up. I do everything for you. I'll get a lawyer and you can leave everything to me." That could be considered undue influence, and those wills rarely stand.

Ideally, families want to fix this situation before the parent dies, but if they find out this breach happened after the fact, it's not necessarily too late. The terms of a will can be changed after the person dies if the family can prove the person who died (referred to as the **decedent** in legal circles) lacked the capacity to write the will, was under undue influence, was weak-minded, or wrote the will under duress.

Cases where someone changed a will while in a compromised state are sadly common. "I've undone a zillion transfers of assets after a person died and we determined that person changed the will under duress, or while weak-minded, or while lacking the capacity to sign a will and trust," Palma said.

Although wills rarely hold up in these situations, that doesn't stop families and neighbors from trying.

Good attorneys will question the circumstance. They will ask, Did the person who died have the capacity to make the decision when they made it? What medications were they taking, and did those affect their mental status? "If you determine that they were not of sound mind when they made key decisions, you file an action to undo the transfers of the will and trust," said Palma.

An acquaintance of mine, an attorney, almost saw this happen in her family. Her husband was one of four brothers. The oldest brother had been married for more than forty years, and he and his wife had no children. The father died, and the mother carried on the couple's agreement that their estate would be divided evenly among their four sons. Unexpectedly, the oldest son died six weeks before his mother died. After his death, the mother told my friend that she wanted that son's wife to get his share of the inheritance "for putting up with him all those years."

My acquaintance suggested the family amend the will. One of the brothers, also an attorney, went to see his mother about this, and reported back that she couldn't sign the codicil (the change to the will) because she "lacked capacity." My friend said she would pay Mom a visit in a few days to see if perhaps she was more lucid.

When my friend paid the visit, the mother was in a fine state of mind. She gladly signed the change to the will, and the widowed wife got her husband's inheritance. The other attorney in the family never mentioned the matter again.

Who's the president?

Not all cases end so smoothly. Both Anthony Palma and Howard Zaritsky have encountered unscrupulous family members who try to work the system to their benefit.

"I've seen families come in with their ninety-two-year-old father," Palma said. "The kids want him to create a trust. I ask him, 'Who's the president? Do you have a rough idea what's in your checking account? Do you own your home, or do you rent? Can you identify your children and give me their names?' If Dad doesn't know the answers, he's not signing a will and trust."

Sadly, what often happens next is those families go find a less ethical attorney who will write this man's will. A better approach if the elderly parent does not have a will and is not in a position to create one is to petition the court and ask for an emergency accounting of all assets by a court-appointed guardian.

Unintended consequences also arise with second and third marriages where the new spouse is not that much older than the kids, and the kids aren't going to get their inheritance until after the new spouse dies—if anything is left.

Howard Zaritsky tells the story of five siblings who got together and hired him after their father died because they thought their stepmother was going to get away with too much of their father's estate. They wanted to know the grounds for contesting the will.

"First," Zaritsky told them, "you have to look at the will." This one was not flawed. In fact, an excellent lawyer had drafted it.

"Second," he continued, "you would have to prove that your father was incompetent or was under undue influence by his wife when he wrote the will. That is difficult to prove because a spouse is supposed to have influence. Also, your dad was a surgeon. If we bring you to admit he was mentally incompetent, all his former patients would have grounds to sue him. I don't think you want to do that."

Of course, the dad could have planned for this, Zaritsky said. He could have talked to the kids rather than have the will be a surprise, or he could have left some money directly to the kids and some in a trust to the wife. But he didn't. Instead, he left it for them to fight about.

The kids aren't always the problem. Palma recalls a case where his firm was suing a local lawmaker who had gotten himself appointed as the trustee of a rich friend who was dying. The judge in town loved the politician, though the dying friend's kids tried to get him out of the picture and get control of the estate. To do that, they wound up paying him $2.5 million to settle the case and make him go away.

"You do want to settle, or these cases can get very expensive," Palma warned. "The problem is, families won't settle. They dig in," which is why, he sardonically added, "these cases are a lawyer's dream."

Living probate

If you think your will could cause a stir or spark a challenge, ask your attorney to help you make it watertight. In a few states—at this writing, Alaska, Arkansas, North Dakota, and Ohio—one tool that can help is **living probate**. This allows you, the author of the will, to ask the court to determine whether your will is valid before you die. This legal action reduces the chances of a successful post-death challenge by a survivor. If the court finds the will is not valid, you can change it so that it is.

So, let's say a woman who has no living children wants to leave everything to her church. But after she dies, her nieces and nephews challenge the will, claiming the church pressured her. Who's to say? A living probate would solve it.

"More states should allow this," Zaritsky said. "You go to court. You say this is my will. A judge asks you a few questions, declares the author is of sound mind and under no undue influence, and that's that. The will is valid, and the heirs can't contest it."

In the other states, you have to die before you know whether your will holds up.

But since most people don't have wills in the first place (a fact that is going to change after this book, right?), few ever get this far.

It all gets back to where we started, Palma said. Know how the assets are titled, to whom they're supposed to go, and where they're located. After you address that whole first tier, then on that you build your wills and trusts, created when parties are of sound mind. And you make them ironclad with fences of protection.

"I've been doing this for forty years," he said, "and what I know is that you had better prepare for the worst. The most honest people in world become awful when money is involved."

But Mine's Fake and His Is Real

Innocent mistakes happen, too, as in the case of property that turns out not to be as valuable as once thought. For instance, what happens if an asset, like a piece of fine jewelry, isn't worth what the will says it's worth? Say a surviving parent leaves her daughter a family diamond ring that the will states is worth $20,000. But along the way someone switched the stone, so it's only worth its weight in gold, maybe $200. Thinking she was evening out the gifting, the same parent left her son a classic Mercedes convertible that really is worth the $20,000 she claimed it was. How does the estate reconcile the difference?

"In cases of value discrepancy, the personal representative for the family should get the items professionally appraised for market value, and then have the estate even out the difference by paying the one who was shorted the difference," said estate lawyer Anthony Palma.

He also advises extreme specificity and vigilance if valuable items might be fodder for a fight. Know where the items are and protect them.

"Families fight over everything!" Palma said. "They fight over the salt and pepper shakers."

You have to be specific, experts say. Even when you are specific about who gets what, those contested items have a way of disappearing, and no one can find them.

Palma's advice regarding jewelry: "Put the diamond ring under lock and key and don't let it come out without supervision and a court order."

No-contest clauses

Another option available in some states is a no-contest clause, which you can include in your will to stop challenges. The clause basically says to anyone unhappy with their share, go ahead and challenge the will, but if you file any action, you get nothing.

Part Four

THE MAGIC FUNNEL

What we do for ourselves dies with us.
What we do for others and the world remains and
is immortal.

—**ALBERT PIKE**, American author (1809–1891)

Leaving a blessing not a burden starts with getting your papers in order, but the effort shouldn't stop there. The real mess, as anyone who has cleared out a parent's home will tell you, lies in all the stuff. In this section we'll get a handle on what it's all worth, and how to convert material belongings into money, and ultimately into meaning.

CHAPTER 16

Turning Material Goods into Money, Then into Meaning

What to do with everything else

L et's look back at where we've been. We began talking about reality, about facts of life we need to face whether or not we want to, and we laid the groundwork for why we need to plan. We learned a whole new vocabulary that comes with such planning. We took time to think about what's most important to us. We met inspiring individuals who left thoughtful legacies that will continue to make a difference over time. Then top legal and financial experts helped us better understand the tools that allow us to take care of those we love, and maybe some causes, too—as well as some traps to avoid.

Now we come to . . . everything else.

Indeed, a significant part of *leaving the legacy you want* involves having your papers and so-called affairs in order.

When thinking about their estate planning, most people focus on how to manage their financial assets—retirement funds, investments, trust funds, and real estate holdings—so that the dominoes fall just the way they want them to when they die. While not insignificant, the handling of those assets is only half the battle.

Although not exactly "easy," you can manage most of these tasks on the phone, at your desk, or around a conference table. Where the heavy lifting comes in, sometimes literally (that heirloom armoire!), falls in the "everything else" category.

When figuring out *what to do with everything you own to leave the legacy you want*, you also need to look at *all the stuff* that doesn't fit in a folder.

See, we are so much more than our financial assets. We are our dishes and clothes, our books and tools. We are our mementos and music and art and jewelry. We are our collections and decorations and linens and cars. We are our furniture and recipes and photos and diplomas. We are the fruits of our work, and of all we've made by hand, and touched, and loved.

Everything else includes the contents of your house, garage, shed, attic, basement, boat, and barn. These material possessions, the real stuff of life, are the ones most destined to burden your successors. These belongings trip memories, feelings of obligation, and sometimes arguments.

We need to take all that into account and deal with our belongings while we're very much alive and well, and to do this out of respect and fairness so we don't eventually leave our loved ones a mess. "If all you found in an estate was cash, then it would be easy," joked trusts and estates attorney Howard Zaritsky when we got to talking about the stuff.

In the chapters ahead, we will explore what do to with our valuables so when the time comes that we're no longer around to appreciate them, we have arranged to put them in the hands of those who will, or to convert the items into cash to go to a good cause—or both.

But first, to prepare the way, let's look at why we get attached to objects, and how we can begin to let go.

Why we get attached to stuff

What I am going to advise here is so forehead-smackingly obvious and practical, you'll wonder why everyone isn't lightening up and purging as they live. I'll tell you why. It's because we get attached to stuff. It's human nature and it begins when we're babies.

Because mom or dad can't always be around (darn it), babies often find something soft and reassuring to hold on to in their place, like a blanket or a stuffed animal. These security objects are wonderfully comforting, and kids endow them with all kinds of meaning.

Now, my friends, I hope you're sitting down. We never stop doing this. We continue to endow inanimate objects with (arguably irrational) meaning. We just get more sophisticated about it. The dress a woman wore when she met her husband is no longer just a dress, but a garment that shimmers with the memory of a magical moment. The wedding china your family dined on as they gathered around the dinner table during special occasions becomes a symbol of family unity and tradition. Some people connect intensely with their cars, which represent hard work, success, status, and identity.

Though intellectually we know these objects are just a dress, a set of dishes, a car, emotionally they mean much more. Embedded with sentimental value, these objects have become entwined with our stories, our memories, ourselves. Separating real value from sentimental value becomes as difficult as separating sparkle from a diamond.

Streamline Your Life

Although understanding why we get attached to stuff can help us detach, let go, lighten up, and move forward with less—it really is just stuff—letting go becomes even easier if you adopt the right mindset. As you thin out your home and fatten your wallet, you may even start to enjoy the process. Here are some overarching guidelines that will help you break the task down, have a plan, and not get overwhelmed.

- **Make regular purging a lifestyle, not a one-time effort.** Life is not one big contest to see how much you can accumulate—but a peek inside some American homes would have you think so. Edit your belongings as you live, so you have only what you need, use, and love, not what is clogging up your cupboards, closets, and carports. I am not telling you to erase your past, nor am I suggesting that you let go of beautiful possessions that lift your spirits, warm your heart, and delight your eye. I am suggesting that you shed as you grow and move through the phases of your life. Enjoy everything you need, use, and love. It's the rest of your stuff I'm asking you to reconsider. The lighter your living footprint, the smaller your legacy burden.

- **Toss, donate, sell.** Make frequent trips to the donation center. Have a garage or yard sale. Sell stuff online. Depending on where you live, Craigslist can be a good online resource for selling used furniture locally, so you avoid shipping. (Be sure to deal only with local buyers who pay in green cash.) Others have luck selling household goods through Facebook Marketplace, or by using their Nextdoor app. For higher-end items, contact a consignment store, which will sell the item for you and keep a percentage. For really high-end items, look for auction houses in your area. They are equipped to market items and sell to buyers and collectors around the world. (You'll read more about auctions in the next chapter.)

- **Use this mantra.** "Letting go of the past lets you live in the present and makes room for the future."

- **Ask loved ones what they want.** Then either give them the item or leave it to them in your will. To ensure that certain desired possessions go to the specific family members, friends, or causes you want, say so in your will or trust. Don't just say it to someone in passing. Talk really is cheap in this case.

- **Don't assume your kids (or anyone) wants your stuff.** Ask if they want it. If they say no, believe them. "To my amazement, neither of my sons want the cellar full of shop equipment and Craftsman tools that I so carefully acquired over forty years," a reader of my weekly newspaper column once wrote. "They prefer to have a few tools and to hire a handyman when they need something done." Yup! And very few kids want your old brown furniture. It's not personal.

- **Find an appreciative home.** If no one wants an item of value, arrange for the item to go to a worthy home. This next section will explore how to do all that. For everyday items that have market value, like exercise equipment or stereo components, sell them online. You can also usually find takers for scrap wood or fabric from old carpentry or sewing projects. Although finding that right taker or buyer takes effort, when you do, you've discovered downsizing at its best.

- **Know what you have.** Don't guess. Don't delude yourself. And don't leave a tall worthless promise. Identify what you consider "valuable," including precious jewelry, artwork, or collectibles, then have a professional assess it. A once-over by an estate appraisal expert can help you know what you have so you can make better downsizing decisions. This expert should be able to identify which items warrant a closer look from an appraiser, so when you leave items to heirs in your will, you can do so evenly and fairly. This way Sally doesn't get the fake Picasso while Johnny gets the classic vintage Thunderbird.

- **Find the right expert.** Niche experts who specialize in genres like china and figurines, couture fashion, jewelry, coins, stamps, antiques, clocks, fine art, and even old farm equipment are available. Find one who specializes in your type of collectible by searching online for certified appraisers, then looking for one who has expertise in your category and arranging for the expert to see the item and appraise it. Ask what the charge is up front. Be aware that no one who appraises a valuable should ever also offer to buy it. In the next chapter, we'll read about liquidation companies and large auction houses that have these experts on hand and how to know when to call them.

- **If you have something of value, like a curated collection of political buttons that no one in your family understands, or a vast collection of record albums, have it appraised and documented.** Make clear to your successors what you want done with the collection, and, if none of them wants it, who should handle selling it.

- **Liquidate all along the way.** This not only gives you knowledge and control over how much an item is worth, but also takes the burden off the kids. When you convert stuff into cash, everything is simpler. The more of your material world you can convert into cash, the easier it will be to divvy up among your heirs or to leave to that meaningful cause I've gotten you thinking about. Most of us don't want our stuff to become the next generation's problem. And it's a lot easier to divide cash than a car. (See chapters 17 and 23 for guidance and suggestions on how and where to sell your belongings.)

- **Downsize now and spare your heirs.** A newspaper reader of my column said this best in an email to me: "My parents made no provisions for their house full of stuff," he wrote. "They believed their kids would enjoy going through everything, recalling wonderful memories and selecting the items they cherished. I strongly recommend against this plan. It can cause fights, it can be a huge burden, and it is plain inconsiderate. It should be your job to downsize your stuff." Amen.

GOOD TO KNOW

To find a liquidator in your area, try going to the American Society of Estate Liquidators' website (aselonline.com) and search for members of this organization by zip code. Once you find a few names, check their reviews and sources.

CHAPTER 17

Going, Going, Gone

*When liquidating home contents,
keep legacy in mind*

---

wish someone would invent a great big magic funnel that
we could pour everything we own—furniture, dishes, cars,
books, jewelry—into and cash would flow out the other side.
Imagine how that would simplify our lives (and deaths). Imagine how much money there would be. (Hint: A lot less than we
think.) What would we do with the booty? Travel? Buy more
stuff? Stick it in our trust? Leave it for the kids? Give it to
charity?

I picture this imaginary funnel working like the sorting hat
in Harry Potter. It would consider each item as it slid through
and assign it a value. The real value, as in what the market
would pay for it, cash on the barrelhead. Not what you paid. Not
what you would buy it for in a store. Not the appraised value

for insurance purposes. Not what you want to believe. But the truth, which can hurt.

That $300 never-worn prom dress? Twenty bucks. Grandma's wedding china? Free to a good cause. Your $2,000 La-Z-Boy massage rocker recliner? You pay $50 for the haul-away fee.

I believe if we had such a funnel, folks' houses would be much leaner and their wallets much fatter. If folks could confidently know the market value of what they have, they would be less worried about "giving" away an item that was "worth something" and could let go in peace.

However, because we often don't know what certain belongings are worth (and maybe we don't want to know for fear of crushing disappointment—my Beanie Babies collection!), and because we don't know who would buy these items or where to sell them, and because we don't or won't take the time to find out, we cling to stuff we should part with. We feel stuck with stuff, so we sit with it. I am guilty of this, too, although I've gotten better.

The magic funnel

Barry Gordon comes as close to a magic funnel as we can get. Gordon co-owns Gordon's Downsizing and Estate Services. Along with his partners, he founded MaxSold, an online auction company specializing in downsizing and estate sales. "We sell everything," he says. And they do, from the spice rack to the family silver.

In 2019, the Toronto-based company, which has locations throughout North America, hosted 6,200 online downsizing auctions. Most events involved selling all the contents of a home, wall-to-wall, but many were relocation auctions that involved downsizing.

Gordon has been in the liquidation business literally his whole life. His dad started an auctioneering company in 1960, the year Barry was born. That company specialized in helping folks auction off farm equipment and livestock. As the younger Gordon got more involved in the business in the late 1970s, the company evolved to include urban downsizing, which is the company's focus today.

"For years, traditional auctions were generally for the elite," Gordon said. "We wanted to bring the nobility of the auction process to people who worked their whole lives to buy and pay for their homes and furnishings."

MaxSold's all-online auctions typically run for a week. The whole process—which involves categorizing and cataloging items, uploading them to the online sales platform, marketing, closing the sales, invoicing, and coordinating pickups—takes about two weeks.

"I like to think we offer a shining light for those in the dark plight of downsizing," Gordon said.

This man knows his stuff. He also knows what stuff is worth. Don't peek, but take a stab at what you think all the contents (not counting cars or boats) of the average home in North America fetches when it's liquidated?

Ready?

Between $3,000 and $10,000, with an average of around $5,000, Gordon said. This is gross value. Generally, in the case of an estate sale that grosses $5,000, after MaxSold takes a 30

> *"I like to think we offer a shining light for those in the dark plight of downsizing."*
> —**Barry Gordon**

percent ($1,500) sales commission plus a $700 management fee, the owner nets $2,800.

"Very rarely—with the exception of a riding lawn mower, car, truck, or boat—do typical households in North America have any items of high value," he said.

I know. Breathe.

Most items we have are not worth nearly what we think they're worth, and certainly nowhere near what we paid for them. But *sometimes*, some homes do have something of high value, and often the owner doesn't know it. Perhaps it's a stack of old baseball cards, an assortment of designer dresses, a unique piece of silver inherited from an aunt, an old painting bought before the artist was famous, an antique clock—all worth taking a second look at. When that happens, Gordon calls on his network of outside experts to make sure the item gets special handling. You'll read more about these specialists just ahead.

The stuff of celebrity

One of those experts is Brigitte Kruse of Los Angeles, who with her husband started Kruse GWS Auctions in 2009. Her wheelhouse is celebrity memorabilia, artifacts from royal and notable families, vintage couture fashion, and the stuff of old Hollywood. She recently sold one of Jimi Hendrix's guitars for $216,000.

"Many people have items of high value in their homes and don't know it," Kruse said. "We have found more surprises in homes of families of mediocre net worth than in homes of wealthier families, where you would expect."

She shares the story of a client who came to her about eight years ago. He had come into a large collection of old pottery. A distant relative had owned it, and the client was the closest living kin. The inheritor didn't know what to make of it all.

"He thought the pottery was just a pile of ceramics from the dollar store," Kruse recalled. Good thing he checked. The collection was in fact a repository of antique native Indian pottery that included many rare items in excellent condition. Kruse sold the collection at auction for $830,000, presumably to someone who appreciated it. That was lucky. For lack of organized planning, this collector's efforts and the national treasure he had acquired and protected almost went to waste. The lesson here is that had this person given more thought to the legacy of his collection, he could have arranged for the money to go to charity instead of some random relative without a clue (and in a moment we'll read about someone who did).

Another one of Kruse's favorite stories is about the time she auctioned off a plane that Elvis Presley had owned. The seller had traded a car for the aircraft thirty years ago, she said. "He had been paying $50 a month to store it in some facility in New Mexico all that time," she said. He knew what he had, but he didn't know how much it was worth. Kruse helped him with that.

To verify the item's authenticity, Kruse called the Federal Aviation Administration, which keeps a complete "biography" of private aircrafts. The FAA traced the plane's serial number to sales documents that bore the signatures of the King and his father. At auction, she sold the plane for just over $500,000. And it didn't even have an engine.

The world is their marketplace

To help homeowners and heirs make sure they're not overlooking possessions of rare value, Duncan McLean, president of Waddington's Auctioneers and Appraisers in Toronto, offers to do what he calls a walkabout—only during the pandemic it was more often a Zoomabout. For about $100, he will look through a person's home for items of value. Usually, he ends up reassuring owners that they are not overlooking anything of great worth, but occasionally he spots an item that warrants a closer look.

"After a family member dies, remaining loved ones worry that they will give something away of high value, so it's best to identify those items, take pictures, and show them to specialists who can give you advice on market value, so you can plan accordingly," McLean said.

A few years ago, an elderly woman in need of money came to see him with her daughter. They brought a pile of pictures of items she had to see if any looked valuable. Nothing stood out. Then the daughter told her mom to show him her cup. Out of her handbag, she pulled out an old carved cup she'd bought years before at a church bazaar for $6 "because no one else wanted it." It caught McLean's interest. His experts examined it and found it to be an eighteenth-century Chinese libation cup. With the woman seated in the fourth row, McLean sold it at auction for $800,000.

"She had no idea," he said. "But for every story like that, I have fifty of folks who think they have valuable items that are not. People have a lot of misconceptions, and more often than not I disappoint them and have to talk them out of the trees. But then at least they know."

Waddington's got its start in 1850, running auction houses in Toronto. "Initially, our business was built on selling off estates," McLean told me. "We have pictures of estate sales from the turn of century. People were downsizing in 1910. We held two auctions a week for decades."

As the market for secondhand furniture began to disappear, the auction house migrated to higher-end valuables. In 2007, Waddington's held its first online auction.

Today, the company has a global reach. When marketing high-end products, the auction house literally knows no bounds. "The world is our marketplace," he said. In 2020 they sent auction items they had sold to forty-nine countries. With the exception of Canadian art, most of what Waddington's sells goes to an international market, which includes buyers in Hong Kong, China, the United States, and France.

"If we relied on the Canadian market for selling our items, we wouldn't last a week," he said. After an auction, couriers are lined up waiting to ship items around the world. Waddington has two approved shippers it recommends and offers buyers help with coordinating shipping. However, arranging for the shipping is up to the buyers, meaning that they are responsible for getting the estimates, scheduling the delivery, and paying for it.

When I mention it . . .

McLean said heirlooms often come his way after a grandparent dies and the family is clearing out the home. "They don't always think about giving a percentage of the proceeds to charity, but when I mention it, many stop to consider what Grandpa would have wanted. When they identify a cause he cared about, we can work with them to distribute proceeds in a meaningful way."

Another way McLean acknowledges the passion behind a collection that someone has spent a lifetime building is by including an essay about the collector in his catalog. That tribute serves as a legacy, which the family appreciates, and also adds to the item's provenance, which buyers care about.

GOOD TO KNOW

If you find yourself hosting an estate sale yourself, you'll likely run into what are known in the world of secondhand-furniture sales as "pickers." They frequent estate sales looking for items they can buy and resell for a profit. They will try to offer you the lowest price, typically about half of what they believe they can resell an item for, so they can cover their carrying costs and still make a profit.

Auctioneers, on the other hand, don't buy your furniture. They try to sell your items for the highest possible price because they work for a percentage. At Waddington's that commission is between 5 and 20 percent. The higher the value of the item, the lower the commission, so for instance, a $50,000 painting might have as little as a 5 percent commission.

Art Lover's Passion
Helps Kids Cope with Cancer

When I spoke to McLean in the summer of 2020, he was getting ready to host "one of the biggest legacy auctions we've ever done," which is saying something for the 170-year-old auction house. All the proceeds from the sale of one man's five-hundred-piece art collection were going to a charity that was dear to him. The donor, Richard LaPrairie, an avid collector who was not married and had no children, was known to say that he did not choose the art, the art chose him. He bought what he loved, with little care for resale value.

And he bought a lot.

"When I first visited the gentleman's condo, it was so full of artwork, I could barely turn around," McLean said. Indeed, the collection filled the staircase, leaving only a narrow path up, and took over the dining room table. Even his bathtub was filled with art. "He had a wide variety, including indigenous Inuit art, flat art, and rare pottery," McLean said.

Upon his death, he wanted the entire collection sold at auction and the proceeds to go to benefit Camp Ooch & Camp Trillium, in Ontario, Canada, a charity that benefits children living with cancer.

According to LaPrairie's obituary, once he discovered the camp, "Richard took a lifelong interest in the programs it provided. He donated his complete estate to this charity and the proceeds will continue to transform children's lives for many years to come."

The camp will use the donation to continue its year-round camp-inspired programs in communities and hospitals across Ontario and at three overnight camps specially designed for kids coping with cancer. The camp also has virtual programs for kids and families living in isolation, wherever they are.

"Before COVID-19, we would have had a big live gala," Mclean said. "But now we will do it over video and Zoom."

The lesson: *If you want to make sure the items you've collected and valued fall into appreciative hands and benefit a worthy cause, consider leaving them to an auction house (talk to them first, as they are quite selective) with instructions in your will specifying that the house sell the collection either as a whole or as individual items, which is usually better, and, after they take their commission, to donate the proceeds to the charity of your choice.*

CHAPTER 18

Giving Away the Farm

There's gold in them there tractors

---

okomis is a small town in South Central Illinois with a population of just over two thousand. Unassuming though it may seem, Nokomis happens to be home to Aumann Auctions, the world's leader in the auctioning of antique tractors and collectible farm equipment. Who knew?

"Antique tractors?" I ask when I get owner Kurt Aumann on the phone. "Is that a thing?" I'm trying to be polite, but am picturing huge, rusty old contraptions cluttering the landscape, creating eyesores in the hayfields.

I am, after all, a city girl.

He lets out a big chuckle and says. "You sound like my wife when I first met her. She was from Mississippi. When I told her I collected antique tractors, she said, 'Nobody collects tractors.'"

Boy, were we wrong.

And, yes, this is a thing. "A Rockwellian kind of nostalgia surrounds old tractors," Aumann said. "Folks who grew up on farms or around agriculture remember the tractors of those days fondly."

Aumann says his auction house sells between 2,000 and 2,500 antique and vintage tractors a year, ranging from old steam tractors to those from the 1970s. They can fetch anywhere from $2,000 to over half a million dollars. Indeed, he sold a 1910 Marshall Colonial tractor in 2019 for $535,500.

When selling old farm equipment, the biggest mistake heirs make is not consulting an expert before they put all of a relative's assets on Craigslist or Facebook Marketplace, he said. "They don't take the time to find out what they have."

The day before we first spoke, Aumann said, a woman had come by who had just inherited her father's tractor collection. A banking professional, she didn't know much about her dad's tractors or their worth. She told Aumann she had once asked her father about the tractors and he'd waved her off, saying, "Oh, don't worry, you're just going to sell them to the first person who comes by." And she almost did. As she was clearing out the family farm, someone came by and offered her $150,000 for all eighteen vintage tractors. She almost accepted, but decided to ask around first.

Good thing. Aumann estimates they will bring in over $400,000 at auction.

Now, please don't interpret this as an excuse to hang on to stuff you don't need; rather, it's a reminder to know what you have before you give away the farm.

The second time I talked to Aumann, he was out in South Dakota visiting three different farms to look over their collectible tractors. Meanwhile, he had three crews working in three other states doing the same. "Our business is really rocking right now," he said. "We've been and are out on the road cataloging."

Many farmers do very well, Aumann said. "But outsiders don't know it because farmers are humble and quiet about their success. Many want to help their community. I run into a lot of situations where farmers decide to literally leave the farm to a church or a cause," he said. "Their kids don't want it."

A John Deere tractor dealer and farmer from Nebraska who asked not to be named is an example. He has collected many old tractors over the years. Now that he and his wife are older, they want to sell them and donate the proceeds to benefit a local Christian school.

Another client, an immigrant who started a window-glazing company that was quite successful, has worked with Aumann over the years. He periodically cleans house, or in his case barn, and has provided merchandise for three Aumann auctions—all to benefit charity. "He has created his own charitable foundation that works like a mini United Way," Aumann said. "He divvies up the proceeds to go to schools, parks, and baseball fields."

But most of his clients aren't so organized or forward-thinking. Many call him from farms in complete disarray, feeling overwhelmed. They have a lot of "salvage," he said. That's his polite word for junk.

Like the woman from Iowa who, the week Aumann and I spoke, called him after her ninety-four-year-old father had moved off the farm and into assisted living. He lived on seven acres, with seven buildings, none of which you could walk into because they were jam-packed, plus a house and a total of—are you ready?—more than three hundred vehicles in various stages of disrepair.

"She's embarrassed by his place," he said, "but it's nothing we haven't seen before."

"I bet he's been doing this since he was ten years old," Aumann said he told her.

"How did you know?"

"I know the type," he said.

Another benefit to having Aumann's team on-site is that they see through the emotional layers that clients can't. "It's very upsetting to watch the home of someone you loved, or even one where you once lived, dismantled. We see it clinically and objectively.

"I'll tell you this," Aumann added. "Whatever plan we come up with to clear out her father's place will be better than her plan. Her plan, she said, was to throw a match on it all!"

Based on prior jobs, he estimates that two thirds of what they find will go to salvage and be sold for scrap. "We will cherry-pick the rest. And sell what's valuable at auction. It's nothing we can't handle."

And instead of a big, dirty mess, the daughter and her dad will have a big, clean check.

Auctioneer to the Stars

When you start your auction career at Christie's in New York, like auctioneer and appraiser Tim Luke did thirty years ago, you see it all. Since then, Luke has been a regular on PBS's *Antiques Roadshow*, appeared on *Cash in the Attic* and *Strange Inheritance*, and been a guest on numerous TV shows, including *Oprah* and *The View*.

Today, Luke, age fifty-six, and his business partner and husband, Greg Strahm, age seventy-one, own and operate TreasureQuest Group, an auction, appraisal, and events company that conducts auctions at many highbrow events from Beverly Hills to Manhattan to Palm Beach. Based in Hobe Sound, Florida, the couple also holds seminars on how the auction and appraisal process works.

He and auctioneer and appraiser Kurt Aumann offer this loud-and-clear takeaway:

- **You are not alone.** Let this story be a parable. However big your mess, someone else has a bigger one, and experts are available to help you out from under it.

- **Find out what you have.** Whether you have inherited a collection of vintage tractors, a pile of old silverware, or a closet full of Chanel suits, if you have the vaguest sense that an item might be valuable, take the time to check it out. A search online for what like items are selling for—if at all—can offer some direction. Be as specific as possible when you search. Also look online for collectors of a category of items, like old crockery.

- **Don't shoot the messenger.** When you seek out a reputable expert, heed his or her advice. They are only trying to help. They have nothing to gain by telling you something is likely worth less than it is.

- **Take the money and run.** Don't think you'll get a better offer. A bird in hand is good. As the real estate maxim goes: Your first offer is usually your best offer. If an auctioneer tells you there's not a big market for what you're selling, don't wait it out.

Another appraiser explained it this way: If you have an antique you think is worth $2,500 and you turn down an offer for $1,500, ask yourself: "Would I buy that antique for $1,500?" Because you just did.

- **Consider the bigger picture.** The furniture market today is pretty saturated. This is the first time in history we have two generations downsizing at the same time: baby boomers and their parents. This era of more supply and less demand has driven values down.

- **Keep your perspective.** "We have seen far too many families fighting over the most inexpensive clock or plate because of sentimental value."

As for Luke and Strahm, they have a will that includes a legacy fund. "We don't have kids, but we do have dogs (cocker spaniels Sienna and Cocoa), so we plan to leave the bulk of our estate to the National Auctioneers Association and the Humane Society. Per our instruction, our art collection is to be sold at auction with instructions for the proceeds to go to these organizations."

CHAPTER 19

Get Real About Value

Market power

Excuses, excuses. Every time the subject of downsizing comes up in a conversation—and with me that's often—the other person has a rash of reasons for dodging the task. This person invariably starts by saying, "I really need to clear out my (fill in the blank: house, attic, storage unit, basement, parent's house, garage, all the above), but . . . " and you know the rest.

While I am not recommending any of us give up items we love to live with or look at, or that we need, use, and love, I am strongly encouraging a serious editing of your stuff.

Yet many of us would rather poke needles in our eyes or eat rats than go through our stuff, much less belongings our parents have left behind. Chief among the excuses is fear you will get rid of something truly valuable and not know it. Right behind that, though you won't admit it, is the worry that you might have to face the fact that what you thought was valuable isn't. You want to cling to your fantasy that those Cabbage Patch dolls you've been hanging on to or that Norman Rockwell mug collection will put your kids or grandkids through college.

You'd better have a Plan B.

So, you close the door on the matter, literally. And stuff sits. I've seen you.

The liquidators at Everything but the House, an online estate-sale marketplace, deal with this conundrum every day. They have niche experts in a dozen specialties, including fine art, antiques, fashion, rugs, coins, sports memorabilia, military medals, even firearms, who can clarify at a glance whether something warrants a closer look or, more often, whether it doesn't. (I know. That hurts.)

Converting stuff to cash

While it's fun to dream that we have heirloom items worthy of a Sotheby's auction, in reality we mostly just have regular stuff. That's the stuff that led Jacquie Denny and her business partner, Brian Graves, to create Everything but the House in 2007. "We saw a gap in the market between high-end auction houses and the guy who sells stuff behind the barn," Denny said. "People had accumulated items that deserved better treatment but didn't warrant a Sotheby's or Christie's auction, she said, referring to the famed high-end auction houses.

An online estate-sale marketplace, EBTH (ebth.com) helps folks downsize, or sell everything in a house from the mop and bucket to the collector car. Similar to MaxSold, EBTH photographs, catalogs, curates, lists, and markets items for online sales. The auctions can involve selling the wall-to-wall contents of a family home or someone's vintage camera collection, which the company markets to buyers in 113 countries, putting the collection in front of more than two million sets of registered eyeballs, Denny said.

"I'm working right now with a daughter who inherited her dad's political button collection," she said. "She didn't know which ones were worth $5 or $5,000. We're in the process of cataloging those."

EBTH charges commissions on a sliding scale from 20 percent for items that sell for $1,000 or more up to 50 percent for items that sell for below $150.

When the company's professionals first assess a house, they divide items into three categories, Denny said. About 60 to 70 percent of the contents are saleable. The rest goes into the donation pile (where the write-off value usually exceeds the net sale) or the disposable pile. They also put aside items they suspect could fetch a nice price. They send a photo of those items or collections to experts in that genre to find out whether the item would benefit from special handing.

Then the online auction-style sale begins, with bids starting at a dollar. Although EBTH's main business is to liquidate entire households, the company will also do single high-end items, using an open auction platform unhindered by location and targeting collectors.

Now, please pour yourself a sobering cup of coffee and listen. Here's what doesn't matter:

- How much you paid for an item.

- How much you love it.
- How much it's selling for on eBay.

"There's a lot of sentimental value out there," Denny said. "People get really upset when they learn that something they treasure isn't worth much."

What does matter is the market, the market, the market. "When everyone wants that one thing, that is where the buying power is," said Denny. You cannot control that. Sorry.

When you're ready to find out what your stuff is worth, start with Google. Search for how much items like yours have sold for online, not what they're selling for. Asking prices are meaningless. A better indication of market value is how much the items sold for.

If you think you have a truly valuable item, consider paying someone to appraise it, Denny said. (See chapters 5 and 17 for more on working with an appraiser.) With an appraisal in hand, you can sell it yourself.

Like others in the estate-selling business, Barry Gordon of MaxSold often has to deliver the disappointing news that something a client treasures or collects isn't worth much. Common examples, he said, include Blue Mountain Pottery, Franklin Mint plates, and Hummel or Royal Doulton figurines. Although called "collectibles," they have become substantially less valuable over time. "They're not junk," Gordon says, "but they're not valuable."

Now, if you've collected Prada bags or antique farm tractors, then yes, you need to talk to a high-end auction house that specializes, he said.

Denny's best advice for those who want to leave their families with a blessing not a burden is to have a plan. "Families need to have a plan and to communicate it in a family meeting and a written will."

Can I get an amen, sister?

"Unfortunately, while everyone thinks that's a great idea, most never get around to it." (We know, but we're changing that, right?) "Don't wait for your parents to initiate the talk. Ask them what they have that you should know about," Denny said. "Know where the sterling silverware is."

Instead, what she more often sees happen is one partner dies and the surviving spouse is overwhelmed. Their three children all live in different parts of the United States. The one who lives closest puts all the household contents in a dumpster. The siblings get mad and say it was all worth a million dollars. And relationships sour from there.

"If families have the forethought to identify us in their wills and specify that we're to sell the contents of the home and give the proceeds to the executor or trustee to divide equally among the kids, all these hard feelings and accusations could be spared," she said.

What's Hot (and Not) in the Secondhand Market

To find out what buried treasures might be lurking in the average home, I tapped several EBTH experts and asked what the most surprising hot sellers in their categories were, as well as what the duds were, knowing that what's hot changes with the times. Here's what I learned:

- **Furniture**

    Surprise! One category that often amazes folks when they discover its value is midcentury modern furniture, said John Neiheisel, general art and antique specialist at EBTH. Before you haul that chair from the 1960s off to the Goodwill, have it appraised. EBTH recently sold a Lane coffee table after a design of Andre Bus for $825.

    Sorry . . . Those "collector" items popular in the '70s, '80s and '90s, which implied their value would only increase, are a bust. Due to the mass production and wave upon wave of these items coming to market, the value of almost anything sold with the moniker "limited edition" has fallen off greatly. When we spoke, he had just sold six Franciscan Masterpiece collector's plates, three Gorham Norman Rockwell mugs, and a bushel of Ty Beanie Babies for $1 per lot.

- **Fashion**

    Surprise! Look no farther than your closet for hidden gems, said EBTH's fashion and accessories expert. Handiwork and history are the heavy hitters. Vintage items that were made well with quality craftsmanship and good materials could fetch a handsome ransom: Those 1960s' Levi's 501 jeans, your dad's Lucchese cowboy boots, and Grandma's Lucite handbag are examples. Pendleton wools are also highly coveted.

    Sorry . . . That dress you recently paid $500 for new and those big-ticket shoes depreciated the minute you got them home. They don't bring much of a return unless they're by a top designer.

- **Coins and Stamps**

    Surprise! Uniform buttons, including rare Civil War–era buttons, and patches can fetch over a thousand dollars each, says Anton Bogdanov, coin, currency, and stamp specialist for EBTH. Today, a strong market exists for early US military insignia, and especially for Army Air Force squadron patches.

Sorry . . . Old coins are more common than you'd expect. A combination of factors, including rarity, demand, and condition, will determine their auction value. A coin's age will rarely have any effect on price, said Bogdanov. You can buy the most common varieties of ancient Greek and Roman bronze coins for under $20 apiece.

- **Sports and Memorabilia**
  Surprise! Some of the most valuable sports memorabilia are baseball cards and bobbleheads, according to Ben Morrill, sports and memorabilia specialist. Early twentieth-century cards from between 1930 and 1960 can attract a nice price due to the low number of Hall of Fame player rookie cards released in the early 1950s, like the 1955 Roberto Clemente rookie card and the 1954 Hank Aaron rookie card. Bobbleheads from the early 1960s can bring anywhere from $75 to $145 dollars depending on the team and the piece's condition.

  Sorry . . . Baseball cards from the 1980s and 1990s are a bust. These cards' value fell after Topps, the sole producer of baseball cards from 1956 to 1980, ended its monopoly. From 1981 on, other manufacturers like Donruss, Upper Deck, and Fleer flooded the market. The high volume of cards lowered their value.

Now you try. What's worth more?

- A group of fifty-eight copper and bronze ancient Roman Imperial coins, including a coin from Constantine the Great dating to approximately 200 to 400 BCE
- A collection of 1930s to 1950s baseball cards with such cards as 1933 Goudey, Diamond Stars, National Chicle, and Play Ball cards, 1935 Goudey Four in One, 1949 Bowman, 1951 Topps, and more

---

Answer: The coins sold for $51 total. The card collection sold for $785.

CHAPTER 20

Deborah's Mom: Keeping the Stories Alive

Downsizing through the decades

"I'm up to my eyeballs in needlepoint pillows," came the text from my neighbor and friend Deborah Robison when I asked how her mother's move was going. "I'm decluttering generations of inheritance."

I have been there, and now Deborah is. Going through a parent's belongings is a rite of passage almost none of us avoids. A task that seems straightforward on the surface grabs you by the ankles and drags you under with the uncompromising pull of a riptide. Deborah is standing on that proverbial shore. Our parents could have made this so much easier on us, I'm thinking for the ten-thousandth time, and Deborah's mom happens to be one of the more thoughtful ones.

"I just found Mom's baby shoes" came the next text. "They button up and are 97 years old!"

In she goes.

At age ninety-eight, Deborah's mother decided to move from her one-bedroom apartment to a smaller place in a Florida community that offered more senior support.

"The move was all her idea," Deborah said the next day as we went for a walk with the dogs. "Mom has always been forward-looking and organized. And she loves the new place. The support makes her feel more secure."

More parents like this, please.

"She's just worried that clearing out her apartment will be too much trouble for me," Deborah added, waving her hand as if swatting at a minor nuisance. "No, Mom. No trouble at all!"

And we laughed.

The apartment, of course, tells a different story. The packed-up place is full of heavy old furniture, antiques, artwork the grandchildren made, and more than two dozen needlepoint items—covered stools, chair seat covers, pillows, wall hangings—made by Deborah's grandmother. Colored Post-it notes dot the furniture and boxes like confetti.

"Each color indicates where the pieces are going," said Deborah, the ringmaster of this three-ring circus. The blue stickie items are going on a truck heading from Florida to Pennsylvania, where they'll be divided among family members. "Mom has already decided whom she wants to have what. I'm just executing her wishes."

Again, more parents like this, please.

Monday another truck will pick up everything else and make four drops locally:

1) Mom's new, smaller place, 2) Deborah's house, 3) the consignment store, and 4) the donation center.

"The stuff that gets off the truck last goes in first," said Deborah, a recently retired marketing executive. Overwhelming as these logistics are, I knew from experience that this was the easy part. I didn't tell her that, although she was starting to see that for herself.

"I had no idea how submerged I would get. I thought I was going to just pack and ship, but that was the least of the work. I didn't expect to take such a deep dive into the family history."

"Umm-hmm."

"I am walking that line between preserving the family history and not perpetuating the avalanche that compounds with each generation," she said. "I mean, I have three sets of china."

Is everyone out there listening?

"Fortunately, Mom is a great resource and can tell me why certain items have significance."

"Wait," I interrupt. "Do you know how lucky you are to have a mom who not only has a plan, but who also can remember the family history?"

She knows.

Lessons Learned from Downsizing Mom:
From Biggest Shock to Best Advice

Always curious about how smart, thoughtful people navigate these waters, I asked Deborah about the highs, lows, and findings of her downsizing journey.

- **Biggest shock:** "How many keepsakes my mother had. She saved every birthday and Mother's Day card ever sent to her. That was overwhelming."

- **Biggest burden:** "When you inherit items that previous generations have placed great value in, it becomes instilled in you that these pieces have value—but they often don't. You feel a responsibility to find a good home for the piece and balance that against the reality that you really don't want to keep it in your house." Amen. I believe we've covered that, yes?

- **Best resource:** Online outlets, like Craigslist, offer more avenues to sell furniture quickly without relying on consignment stores, which are often selective. "Selling a piece to someone who really wants or needs it gives you the satisfaction that you've done right by the piece and by your parent," Deborah said.

- **Best idea:** Because she didn't want to ship items to relatives and hand pieces down to her twenty-seven-year-old twin daughters without context, she gathered facts with her mom's help and typed notes to send along. Notes included details about the original owner, and when and why the item was used. For example, Deborah's great-grandmother became a widow in the early 1900s. To support herself and her two young children, she opened a general store in Philadelphia. Customers used brass scoops to get items sold from barrels. Deborah now has one of the scoops. "Until you know how she came to open the store and why, the scoop is pretty meaningless."

- **Best advice:** Talk to family elders now, while their stories are still alive. Deborah learned that her paternal grandmother needlepointed all those items to calm her nerves while both of her sons, including Deborah's dad, were fighting in World War II. "Each family member will get a pillow, which some are more enthusiastic about than others," she said. The point being, an object means more when it's connected to a story, and a story means more when it's connected to an object.

- **Most unexpected finding:** Family members differ on how much or little they want. Some want many items; others want few, she said, confirming what I've long preached: How much you want of someone's possessions has no correlation to how much you loved them. And don't assume a relative wants an item. Ask.

- **Biggest takeaway:** Cull as you live rather than postpone the inevitable. "This has motivated me to pare my things down, starting with my crystal," Deborah said. "Once I get through Mom's stuff, my stuff is next."

The lesson: Any adult child who has cleared out a parent's home (my hand is up) knows how enormously difficult the job is. Make this easier on your kids. Document what needs context, then make selling, donating, tossing, and otherwise purging as you live a way of life.

CHAPTER 21

That Paper Trail

*What to do with diplomas, certificates,
and the family photos*

H*i Marni, I'm usually pretty good at decluttering and getting
rid of things, but something is holding me back,* said the email
from a reader of my weekly newspaper column.

*My husband recently passed away. He was well-known in his
field, and now I'm faced with LOTS of diplomas and certificates that
we'd had professionally framed and put in his office. It always made
him happy to see them, but eventually he ended up putting them in a
(huge) box and they sat in our garage for 5–6 years before he died. I
don't need them for any reason I can think of, but I hate to get rid of
them in case there's a reason for keeping I don't see. I've been thinking about perhaps just taking photos of them all and giving away the
frames. I guess I could keep the actual papers in a file, but I would
prefer not to unless I should. Any thoughts?*

Betty, Celebration, Fla.

At some point all of us will face (or have faced) Betty's diploma dilemma. While I have my opinion, which we'll get to, I ran the loaded question by three decluttering experts.

- Professional organizer Sue Marie Bowling said, "Guilt can compel us to keep things for the life we lived, not the life we are living." (Let that sink in for a minute.) "Your reader seems to have little emotional attachment to the *physical* evidence of her husband's achievements. She journeyed through those accomplishments with him, so [she] has the memories. However, for the rest of her family, a digitized record of her husband's accomplishments would suffice and help ensure that they are not lost to history."

- Mitch Goldstone, owner of ScanMyPhotos.com, recommends scanning *and* saving the originals. "These precious records hold value to more than the person who earned them," he added. "They are more than a bragging right. They are part of your family's history and should be preserved." Note: If you are going to save these paper pieces of history, remove them from their frames, insert them in acid-free page protectors, and store them in an archival-quality box in a place that won't get too hot (so not the attic) or flood (so not the basement).

- Interior designer Mark Brunetz, the author of *Take the U Out of Clutter*, had this suggestion: "As a tribute to her husband, Betty should upcycle the certificates. Commission a local artist or art student to take the most meaningful certificates and create a mixed-media piece of art that reflects the wife's current style of décor. This way, they can be admired daily in a whole new way." And you have just one framed piece, not ten.

All good advice. However, to really resolve what's at the core of the diploma dilemma, we need to dive a little deeper. My test for what to save and what to let go of boils down to three questions: Do I *need* it? Do I *use* it? Do I *love* it? You must answer yes to at least one.

So, if I apply my need-use-love formula to the diplomas and important papers, here's how that would shake out.

I would save birth, death, and marriage certificates because you might need them, and they matter in genealogical records. Academic diplomas are arguably useful only as long as the person is alive, the same way a driver's license is useful. My degrees expire when I do. My family has my permission to toss them when I'm gone.

Solving the Diploma Dilemma

Here are some other considerations when working through that pretzel knot of whether to keep a loved one's diplomas:

- **Whose is it?** These diplomas aren't yours. If the person who earned it has died, the degree is not going to benefit anyone else. Yes, it represents an accomplishment, but the person's lifework is a testament to that. Letting go of the physical symbol does not erase the achievement, nor does it diminish your love or respect for that person.

- **Play it forward.** Ask yourself, *If I don't deal with it, who will?* Often our decision to hang on is merely thinly disguised procrastination. Not dealing with stuff is a way of dealing with it. "We'll just put it in a box and let the kids decide." That is how the giant generational snowball of stuff rolls forward, growing and weighing down those we least want to burden. Now your kids have to deal with the pile of procrastination and feel obligated not to break the chain. Is that what you want?

- **Does it prove something that can't otherwise be proven?** Colleges keep records of their graduates. If there was ever any doubt that a family member got a degree from a particular institution, you could find out.

- **Is this an exception?** Certain diplomas do have historical significance. If they belonged to, say, someone who became a Supreme Court justice, or walked on the Moon, or was the first person in your family to graduate from college, or if it was signed by someone famous, then you might have something worth hanging on to.

- **Would saving it make a difference?** Call me unsentimental, but I do not need to see my grandma's high school diploma. When I came across my mother's bachelor's degree in nursing diploma after she died, I took a long look at it, thought about her life and her nursing career, and let it go. Did I scan it? No. Did I put it in an archival box? No. Do I love her less? No. Do I appreciate less the fact that she modeled for me how to have a profession and a family? No. That is all in me, and in my girls. Should you do what I did? Probably, but the decision is yours.

Betty, your husband already telegraphed that his diplomas had served their purpose. When his career wound down, he boxed them up. You answered your own question: "I don't need them for any reason I can think of." And you are right. Scan or photograph your husband's most important diplomas *only* if that will make you feel better. Don't be afraid to let them go. It's really OK.

Saving old photos and documents

"You still have boxes of Mom and Dad's stuff?" I twist my finger in my ear to make sure I'm hearing clearly. I'm on the phone with my brother, who's three thousand miles away in California. Good thing, or I might have to once again fill his belly button with glue while he's sleeping. He's moving, prompting this confession to his sister, the purge queen.

Our parents have both passed on, Mom most recently, in 2016. Now, almost four years later, Craig tells me he's been holding on to boxes of their stuff, keeping them at his office, because "I can't bring myself to go through them."

Great. Here I thought we were done. A few years before Mom died, I cleared out our family home, where my parents lived for nearly fifty years, when they moved into assisted living. The effort required a bulldozer, smelling salts, an iron stomach, a therapy dog, and the stamina of a triathlete.

"There's more?" I still couldn't believe it.

He texts me a picture of ten bankers' boxes stacked and neatly labeled. I'd be coming to California in a couple months, I told him, and I agree to set aside an afternoon to deal with the boxes.

At my brother's architecture firm, I find the boxes stacked in the model shop. I have plenty of room to unpack, sort, and toss. I brush my palms together, ready to make short work of this project, and summon a large trash bin. I make stations: trash, scan, donate, keep.

I crack open box one. Ah, geez, all photos. That will take forever. I push it aside and move to box two, hoping to get some momentum going. It's worse. Soon I am flooded, physically and emotionally, with images and documents of my parents' lives before kids, before each other. Mom's college term papers. Their vaccination records. (Mom, always the public-health nurse.)

I find commendations from Dad's days in the marines, his work history, beginning with his offer letter from the engineering firm where he worked for thirty years (starting hourly pay: $1.75), the photo album of his retirement, a book of his patents.

What am I supposed to do with all this?

By turns, I am laughing like a monkey troop, welling up like a homecoming queen, and reading as soberly as a Supreme Court justice. Five hours later, my brother interrupts my reverie to remind me of our dinner reservation. He looks around the formerly tidy model shop, now ransacked.

"I'm not going to finish," I confess, looking sheepish.

Craig looks at the six unopened boxes. His mouth makes a taut seam.

"I need another full day, at least, probably two," I concede.

So much for my plan to plow through the boxes in one afternoon and send an edited pile of photos to ScanMyPhotos.com, where high-speed scanners reduce mountain heaps of snapshots into easy-to-access digitized images.

The scanners were working overtime because that weekend, the country had just had a rash of hurricanes and wildfires. "Times like these make people realize all can be gone in a flash," says owner Mitch Goldstone.

I've called Goldstone to tell him about the mess I'm in. He gives me a pep talk. "Every day I see photos and documents

> *Orderliness is a blessing you leave your children. Again, it's not just what you leave, but how you leave it that matters.*

destroyed by mildew, moisture, high temperatures, dirt, and bugs. Those old storage boxes will just disintegrate," says Goldstone, whose company scans three hundred thousand photos a day, which is nothing when you consider that Americans have 3.5 trillion analog photos sitting in shoeboxes taking up storage space and risking permanent loss.

However, beyond the ravages of nature, an even bigger enemy of all family photos and historical documents is procrastination.

If you don't sort out, save, and subtitle, your kids won't. And that's your legacy.

Who from the next generation will see (and there's a limit to what they'll want to see) the college diplomas, the honorable military record, the birth certificates, the passage papers of your grandparents entering this country—in short, your family's legacy—if you don't pull these documents together, decide what matters, and save them for posterity?

He likes to suggest that families go through the photos during family get-togethers to create stacks to digitally save and share with family members. "Sharing old stories will be a lot better than talking about politics," he said.

Making Memories
Out of a Mess

When faced with a mountain of paper memories, here's how to sort and save:

- **Start with the photos.** Select those you want; organize them by year and event. (I tossed all photos of landscapes, people I didn't know, and duplicates.) Write on an index card "Halloween 2007." Secure the card to the photo bundle with a rubber band. (The card gets scanned, too.) Goldstone's company will provide a self-addressed, shoebox-size container that holds 1,800 photos, which costs $145 to scan.

- **Sort important papers.** Old letters and certificates are often too fragile to scan. For those, grab your smartphone and take pictures, says Goldstone. Batch photos on your phone, then save them, along with your DVD of scanned photos, to your laptop, thumb drive, the cloud, and Google Photos. Mobile scanning apps such as Adobe Scan and Genius Scan let you scan a picture of a document with your phone and convert the image to a PDF. Send copies to family members, and keep a backup off-site.

- **Verify capture.** Once old photos and documents are scanned or photographed, verify that the images are properly saved and preserved in multiple places. Then—deep breath—you can toss the originals. Although this idea always makes my stomach fall like an elevator in a mine shaft, Goldstone is right. Scanned and tossed is saved, not lost. Moreover, scanned and stored is preserved, and, once archived, the quality will keep.

- **Toss everything? Just about.** Hold on to only the most important keepsakes, that letter that still smells like your mom's perfume, or that black-and-white portrait of your father in the cardboard folder with the deckled edge. But beware the temptation to cling to too much.

- **Plan for digital migration.** Anyone who remembers floppy discs knows how technology changes. To protect against "digital rot," save images in several formats so data can always be retrieved and moved to the next generation of technology or relatives.

If you're going to die, be orderly about it

A friend once told me that her mom (who lived to be ninety) often used to say, "I'm getting my drawers in dying order." I love that line. It's not morbid. It's thoughtful. Here is a woman thinking about the impact her belongings, and how she leaves them, are going to have on those after her, what those sweeping up after she's gone will have to contend with, whether she lives to a ripe old age or gets hit by a meteor.

I've started to use that saying—getting my drawers in dying order—as my lens, too. I go beyond drawers, of course. When I look at my garage, my pantry, my closets, my office files, I ask, "What would it be like to come upon this and sort it all out? Is this the best I can do?"

Orderliness is a blessing you leave your children. Again, it's not just what you leave, but how you leave it that matters.

I think of how my mom used to tell me to make sure I always wore clean, nice underwear in case I got hit by a bus. This used to puzzle me, conjuring pictures of emergency personnel worrying about the safety pin in my bra instead of my blocked airway, but ultimately I realized that the value Mom was really instilling was about more than the state of my undergarments. She was teaching me to make sure those places no one usually sees are proper and pulled together and reflect well on us, because someday, we never know when, they will be in full view.

CHAPTER 22

To Deal with Collections, First Understand the Collector

From cameos to comic books,
model trains to snow globes

I am about to get myself into trouble—again. A few years ago, while speaking at a book event about what to do with our stuff and our loved ones' stuff, a woman in the audience shared that she and her husband, both pharmacists, had a plan. They had amassed a collection of mortars and pestles from around the world, and upon their deaths, they wanted to have these sets handed out as funeral favors.

OK, so that's weird on a few levels, and it's their death, not mine. But I suggested that maybe she keep the collection intact and donate it all to a pharmacy school.

Bad advice, I later learned. I'll tell you why in a minute, but first let me tell you where my instinct to keep the collection together came from.

Shortly after my aunt, my mother's sister, died, her daughter, my eldest cousin, decided to distribute place settings of our maternal grandmother's china among the grandchildren. This would have been a lovely notion—if we'd wanted it. I loved Grandma Mac, but her old-fashioned flower-festooned china not so much.

Assuming I would want it, however, my cousin gave me two place settings. Eventually, I could give one setting to each of my daughters, she said. (Oh, they'll love that!)

"It's called Forget Me Not," my cousin told me wistfully.

I accepted it graciously, of course, and appreciated the sweet sentiment. But I have china, and I have my mother's china. Now I have these two one-offs of a pattern I would never pick out. If you think about it, there is no end to the cascade of generational china. I tucked my tongue in my cheek, and the china in the closet.

When my brother, who is married with no children, got his place setting, he thought, reasonably, *What am I going to do with this?* Not knowing the backstory, he wrote a tactful email asking our cousin if she could suggest someone else in the family who would like his place setting, who might appreciate it more?

You see where this is going. I get a call from my brother. I get a call from my cousin. I referee my cousin's good intentions to fairly disperse this "family asset" and my brother's desire to reunite the collection—elsewhere.

Because my instinct was that the china was probably more valuable together than apart, and that it should all go to one relative who would appreciate all of it, I suggested the pharmacist keep all the mortars and pestles together, in so many words.

The question haunted me. Although I was dispensing advice,

I still felt as if I were awkwardly groping my way around the topic of collections—specifically the questions of are they better together or apart? Is it all right to break them up?

To rest my mind and my case, I called collections expert Jim Halperin of Dallas, cofounder of Heritage Auctions, one of the nation's largest auction houses, which is known for selling collections, and learned I was wrong about the mortars and pestles—but right about the china.

"Almost every collection is worth more broken up," said Halperin, noting that china, technically, isn't a collection; it's a set, and sets should stay together.

But if you collect paintings from a specific artist, baseball cards, stamps, or dolls, you are going to increase your odds of finding the right buyer—and getting the best price—if you sell them individually.

"Although every collector's dream is to leave their collection intact the way they envisioned it, that's almost always a complete fantasy," he told me.

Halperin, who collects Maxfield Parrish art, superhero comic books, political buttons, and movie lobby cards, says he, too, dreams of selling his collections intact, "but I purge that fantasy from my mind."

How to Liquidate a Collection

I asked Halperin the following questions about collections and busted a few more myths of my making:

- **Are collections better dispersed one item at a time?**

  When you have a group of distinct items—not a set, like china—but a collection such as mortars and pestles, don't bundle them for donation or sale if you can help it. "You will almost always get more by selling one item at a time on eBay or at auction, especially if you find the collector looking for that exact item."

- **What if the entire collection is really valuable?**

  Even if you have a museum-worthy art collection, chances are a museum will want only a few pieces. "The rest of the collection winds up in the museum's basement, where it becomes a source of battle among board members who want to get rid of it but are bound by the donor's stipulation that the collection stay together. It's an anchor around their necks," he said. (I can hear Emily Blaugrund Fox, from the Albuquerque Museum Foundation, clapping all the way from chapter 6.) If you really want to help the museum, let museum officials pick what they want to display, then you sell the rest and give them the money. "Even museums would rather have money than art."

- **What is a collectible, and what isn't?**

  Collectibles are groups of items originally made in quantity, like coins, stamps, and sports cars. Valuable collections contain items that you can't find at the mall. They are rare, in good condition, and desirable.

- **What's the difference between a collector and a hoarder?**

  Most collectors are students of what they collect. They know everything about it. They track what they have and know what they want. They have a plan and organize the collection systematically, cataloging items. Hoarders acquire without direction and don't throw anything away.

- **Does having your collection displayed attractively separate the serious collector from the amateur?**

    No. (I'm wrong again.) Having your collection attractively displayed means you have an eye. It doesn't mean you know what you are doing.

- **What's the best way to dispose of a collection?**

    Ideally, collectors should decide while they're alive to sell items in their collection individually so their kids aren't left trying to sell items they don't know anything about. At the very least, they should chronicle what they have, provide a reasonable appraisal of its value, and offer suggestions as to where to find a prospective buyer. One for my side. We've been over this, right?

What makes a collector a collector?

I'd never understood collectors. What compels some folks to seek out stamps or baseball cards or coins? And I still don't understand how one penny can be worth thousands of dollars. "Because that's what people will pay for it" was the answer I got from one collector. But it's still a penny!

I had always pictured collectors as fusty old men in drab, moth-eaten sweaters holding magnifying glasses and penlights, squirreling away odd artifacts in dark, felt-lined drawers. And I thought they were a little off.

Until recently, when I learned I was one of them.

While talking to Halperin, who makes collections his business, about what legacy leavers should do with their collections, I mentioned, in an offhand, this-isn't-even-remotely-in-the-same-category way the two dozen Swarovski crystal figures I've amassed over the years, not seriously, but just because I like them.

"You're a collector," he declared.

"Am not."

"You're not obsessive like many of us addicts. You may not curate and catalog, or doggedly pursue the hard to get, but make no mistake, you're a collector, a fringe collector."

"How do you figure?" I wanted proof.

"Are all your pieces from one maker?" he asked.

"Yes."

"Would you ever buy a duplicate of one you have?"

"No."

"Do you have their original packaging?"

"Yes." That was weird. I never save packaging.

"Do you remember when it started?" he asked, adding, "Every true collector remembers when they first became smitten."

Do I remember. It was the stroke of the new millennium. I was hosting a New Year's Eve dinner party to ring in the new century. One of my guests brought me a hostess gift, a crystal Swarovski bear holding a champagne glass and a bottle of bubbly.

For reasons I cannot explain, I was utterly captivated by this one-and-a-half-inch dazzling trinket. I set the twinkly bear on my mirrored perfume tray.

Soon, I had two, then three, then five faceted crystal critters on my perfume tray. When my menagerie outgrew the tray, I bought a glass mirrored case with shelves.

I splurged on a Swarovski clown because it reminded me of my playful children. I acquired a seahorse that reflected my

California coastal upbringing. Friends and family caught on to my fancy, and I received more as gifts, crystal figures that symbolized what I did or loved: a typewriter, a gold quill pen in an inkstand, a coffee pot, a puppy, a horse. On a trip to Hawaii, I treated myself to a glittery pineapple. From Amsterdam, I brought home a shimmering tulip.

Each figure came with a story, like the one of two bears, one down on one knee handing a red heart to the other, which DC gave me when he proposed.

When I finished my reverie, Halperin said, "Welcome to the club."

Now I understand.

Later, when I'd circled back for another conversation with MaxSold's Gordon, I somewhat nervously asked about my Swarovski collection? Did it fall in the same category as, say, Franklin Mint plates?

I could have done worse, he told me. "They are a good medium collectible. They're small, which is a plus. (Larger items make less desirable collectibles.) They have been followed by people who like the way they glitter (me), and they have no known fakes."

Why Do We Collect?

From Cracker Jack toys to manhole covers, the passion to collect goes back eons. The reasons are many and varied, according to Halperin, who listed these twelve for starters:

- **Knowledge and learning.** Collectors are curious. They are students of their subject and love learning about it.

- **The quest.** For some, the thrill of the hunt feeds their drive to collect the rare and coveted.

- **Bragging rights.** Many collectors like the feeling of pride that comes with owning something sought after.

- **Control.** Owning and categorizing a group of like possessions makes some collectors feel as if they are bringing order to a part of the world. Like librarians, collectors find satisfaction in arranging, organizing, and classifying.

- **The Darwin effect.** Some evolutionary theorists have suggested that having a collection was a way for early man to attract potential mates, as it signaled his ability to accumulate scarce resources.

- **Philanthropy.** Many great collections are ultimately amassed so the owner can donate the lot to museums or universities for later generations to learn from, appreciate, and enjoy.

- **Nostalgia.** Childhood memories prompt many to collect items that remind them of their youth or some connection to a part of history they care about and want to preserve. Collectors of comic books, Pez dispensers, and Barbie dolls are classic examples.

- **Fandom.** Sports fans may collect memorabilia to express loyalty. The same goes for those who collect items related to Disney or Star Wars or Elvis. (His engineless airplane!)

- **Celebrity connection.** Some collectors gather items that once belonged to famous (or infamous) people because these objects are seen as being infused with the essence of that person, which those in the business call the concept of contagion.

- **Relaxation.** Like home gardening and photography, collecting is a leisure activity that those who pursue it enjoy.

- **Social interaction.** Collectors meet at swap meets and auctions where their shared hobby has formed the basis of many friendships, just as folks in the dog-show circuit bond over breeds.

- **To make money.** Though many collectors lose more money than they make, some exceptions are notable. Halperin tells the story of his friend John Jay Pittman, a middle manager for Eastman Kodak married to a schoolteacher. Pittman studied coins, and invested much of his limited income in collecting them. In 1954, to his family's dismay, he mortgaged his house to travel to Egypt and bid on coins at the King Farouk collection auction. When he died in 1996, his family forgave him when the collection sold at auction for over $30 million.

The lesson: Collectors, don't keep the story of your collection to yourself. Be sure your family knows what you have and particularly what it's worth and to whom. Heirs, you may mock the collector, but don't mock the collection, and don't just dismiss it without knowing fully what you have. By selling key collectibles to interested parties, you can not only assure that they go to a good home, thus respecting their owner, but also reallocate the asset to something else meaningful.

CHAPTER 23

Downsizing the Family Jewels

The stuff of legend, lore, and lawsuits

W hen Christine Gerardi arrives at a client's home, the shoeboxes start coming out of the closets. The boxes contain piles of old jewelry, most worthless, some valuable, a lot in between, and always a bewildered owner who doesn't know what to do with it all.

"No other item in a home is more contentious than family jewelry," says Gerardi, a concierge jeweler (meaning that she works with clients in the comfort of their homes) based in Central Florida.

The family jewels are the stuff of legend, lore, and lawsuits. They carry the family history of love, commitment, milestones, and celebrations. They symbolize the bonding that holds families together.

And because jewelry symbolizes love and money, it also lies at the root of many arguments.

When family jewels are passed down through generations, they can be especially symbolic, and sometimes burdensome, raising the question: Where does our responsibility end? (Do I have to keep this, or can I sell it?) They can also be sorely disappointing. Like when you find out that five-carat sapphire ring of Grandma's that was ceremoniously handed down through three generations of women is a fake.

But that's not going to be the case with any of us, because we are going to get ahead of that train wreck, right?

I met Gerardi through a friend, who'd been slogging through her elderly mother's belongings. Gerardi often meets folks when they're at a low point. "People looking to sell jewelry are often dealing with a death or divorce, or need money," she said.

Although I have been in each of those tough spots, blessedly, I was not the week Gerardi came to my house to walk me through the process of how to sort through the family jewels.

I wanted to know (while I am of clear mind) what to keep for pleasure or posterity, what to sell or toss, and whether I had anything worth anything. In the latter case, I also wanted to know how to separate real market value from wishful-thinking value (and this applies to so much more than jewelry), and how to capitalize on it so that significant jewelry gets either handed down appropriately or properly liquidated.

Notably, the day Gerardi came to my house, she was wearing, she tells me, a Cartier watch (let's agree that's expensive), seven-dollar dangle earrings, and a sterling Van Cleef & Arpels knock-off chain necklace she bought for $100 but would cost twelve times that if it were genuine. All this somehow makes her someone I can relate to.

I spread my mishmash of jewelry on the table between us. I steady myself as the flashbacks hit. I have jewelry from my mom, my grandmother, and, oh my, very long-ago boyfriends. I found tiny gold earrings I wore in high school, my class ring, a sorority pin. Why? Ninety percent of this stuff I never wear and would never wear. But somehow, like so many women of a certain age, I have amassed an entire drawerful of these old jewels because I don't know what else to do with them.

What I do know is that I want to get ahead of this. I want to pour the jewelry through a mini magic funnel and convert much of it to cash and not leave it all to my kids to ferret out.

First, in the interest of downsizing to live better and lighter, I want to get rid of any items that have no meaning or value and that I'll never wear again. The fact is all the jewelry that I wear, or will ever wear, could fit in a box the size of this book. Second, because cash in hand is always better than potential cash, I want to sell anything that does have value, just not to me. Once I know the cash value, or have the cash in hand, I can stick it in the trust for my kids or a cause and not speculate about its market value.

Finally, I want to whittle my jewelry collection down to these categories: Jewelry I want to keep because it has meaning and value, and because I wear it or want to pass it down; and jewelry that has no value but I like it and wear it.

Get real about value

That's where Gerardi can help. First, she explains, most misunderstandings happen when consumers don't know the difference between appraised value and cash value. An *appraisal* gives you a price, generally high, for what it would cost to replace the item if it were lost or stolen. This is useful for insurance purposes. An appraisal typically costs money to have done, and, as with any appraisal, the person who appraises your jewelry should never buy it.

Those who want to know cash value want an *evaluation*. A jewelry buyer can tell you what your jewelry is worth in today's market, and offer to buy items for meltdown value or to resell them as they are. Their offer will be much lower than the appraised value. This is where the rub comes in.

"Customers ask me all the time to give them an appraisal when what they really want is an evaluation. They want to know what I would pay them for the item today," she said. "The difference can come as a shock. Hard feelings arise when someone comes in with a ring that they paid $10,000 for and an appraisal that says it's worth $12,000, and a buyer will only give them $3,200. Yet it happens all the time because 95 percent of jewelry is not worth nearly what people paid, or what people think it's worth."

Much of the value is sentimental. "When people buy a piece of jewelry, they are often buying a piece to mark a precious moment in time, an engagement or marriage, a birthday or anniversary."

Where this comes into play in an estate situation is when someone leaves, say, a diamond necklace in a will to a sister. The sister inherits the necklace and the records, including the receipt showing a purchase price of $6,000 and an appraisal saying the necklace is valued at $8,000. The sister believes she's inherited an asset worth $8,000, which is only true if she insures the necklace for that amount and it gets lost or stolen. But if she were to go to sell it, she'd be in for a rude awakening. Depending on the price of gold that day, a buyer might give her $1,800.

No one committed any fraud here.

The lesson: If you want a loved one to have a specific piece of jewelry, first ask if they would like it and let them know why you would like them to have it. The story is often more valuable than the item. If you have an appraisal or a receipt, be clear that those don't reflect market value so the heir is under no false assumptions. If no one wants the item, do everyone a favor and sell it for cash, saving everyone the trouble and disappointment.

The Jewelry Box: How to Separate Trash from Treasure

Now we can sort, save, and sell. To do that, here's what Gerardi recommends:

- **Have the conversations.** If you don't want to leave a mess to the next generation, and you also want to avoid squabbles after you're gone, ask heirs what they want. Discuss your plans for distributing family jewelry in advance, explain your thinking, and settle any perceived slights. If they say they don't want it, consider selling it yourself and adding the cash to your estate's trust. Before you liquidate any family jewelry, ask family members what they want either now or later. Do not sell anything of value that is already part of a will or that is part of a probate or court case.

- **Make three piles.** With everything on the table, Gerardi divided my jewelry into three groups: costume, sterling, and precious metal (yellow or white gold or platinum). Costume jewelry has practically no value. Keep what you like and will wear, and toss or donate the rest, she suggests. "It doesn't matter if it's a Swarovski crystal necklace that you paid $100 for. It's still costume jewelry. The same goes for sterling, although you may find a market for it online. If a piece has a nice gem in it, chances are it's set in gold or platinum. The gold pile is where the value is."

- **Go for the gold.** In the precious-metal pile, pull out anything you wear and enjoy, that has sentimental value and you want to pass down, or that is from a luxury brand designer, such as Tiffany, Van Cleef & Arpels, or Cartier. (There are many others.) Designer pieces will usually sell for more than their melt value, as much as 25 percent more, especially if they're in good condition. Having the original box and receipt can also boost the sale price. The rest of the precious-metal pile can be converted into quick cash.

  "Buyers are pretty much interested in precious metals—gold or platinum—period," she said. Many customers wrongly assume the stones carry the value. "They undervalue gold and overvalue stones." While some larger gemstones are valuable, many gems are literally more trouble to remove than they're worth. Most diamonds other than center stones are worth little. When buying gold jewelry with stones intact, the buyer will typically pay you for the stone's weight as part of the gold, not more or less.

  Pearls, though often cherished heirlooms, are also rarely worth much, she says. I had a long, thirty-six-inch strand in good condition, which she said she would give me $100 for. The exception would be original pearl jewelry by the luxury designer Mikimoto, which has market staying power.

- **Melt or sell?** Before you sell for meltdown value, consider selling fine jewelry in good condition or designer pieces yourself on eBay or on a consignment site like RealReal.com, which authenticates all products it resells to protect buyers from buying, say, a fake Louis Vuitton purse or a knock-off Tiffany necklace. If you think a piece from a lesser brand might have market value, see if it has a mark, name, or stamp. Search it online to see what it's worth. Some companies will list items for you and handle the transaction and shipping for a fee. Otherwise, consider selling it to a gold buyer.

- **Get three offers.** The value of gold depends on the day, and sometimes the hour. While Gerardi and I were meeting, for instance, gold prices went up $6 an ounce. The price also depends on who's doing the evaluating. Gerardi suggests getting three offers for what they would pay you in cash: ask at an independent jewelry store, a pawnshop, and a place that buys gold. Have someone weigh it and compare their offer with an online gold-to-cash calculator such as cashforgoldcalculator. com. If you're selling gold jewelry, a reasonable offer would be 70 to 80 percent of the market value. If you're selling gold coins, a reasonable offer would be 90 percent of the market value.

- **Why not full price?** A piece of jewelry stamped 14K gold is actually 58.5 percent gold plus an alloy. That is one reason your gold won't sell for the going price of gold per ounce. The day Gerardi and I met, gold prices happened to be at a high point, at $1,763 per ounce of pure gold. Over the past ten years gold prices have fluctuated between $500 an ounce and $2,000 an ounce. An ounce is 28 grams. I had 40.5 grams of gold, most 14-karat, that I could easily part with, about the amount of jewelry it would take to fill a shot glass. Some of the items had gemstones, which were neither large nor fine. I sold the gold to Gerardi for $1,000, about 75 percent of the going market price.

Jewelry buyers also have to factor in their carrying costs (the time they have to sit with a piece) when purchasing jewelry or gems that they plan to resell, not melt. If an item reliably sells well, like round, diamond stud earrings, and Valentine's Day is coming up, they'll pay more, because of demand. But if the diamond is a trendy cut, like a princess cut diamond popular in the '90s but not today, they will pay less.

None of us can control the market. What your jewelry is worth today may be a lot less or more than it will be a year from now due to factors outside your control. When Meghan Markle got married with a three-stone ring, that style catapulted in value overnight. When Ben Affleck gave Jennifer Lopez a six-carat pink diamond, the market for pink diamonds skyrocketed.

- **Chronicle what matters.** Have anything you believe to be of significant value, including any diamonds over one carat, professionally appraised by a person trained to do GIA (for Gemological Institute of America) certifications. The bigger the diamond, the more important that is. Keep a fine jewelry file with receipts, records, photos, and any information of sentimental or historical significance. This would be a good place to name who is to get the item per the will, or how you would like the item liquidated and where the funds should go.

- **Get your story straight.** Gerardi sometimes finds herself in awkward positions—for instance, when she has to tell a family that the diamond in the matriarch's wedding ring is really a cubic zirconia. She's had women come to her wanting to sell the diamonds from their rings and trade them for cubic zirconias because they need the cash. Or a husband tells his wife he's going to have her ring cleaned and swaps the stone. Imagine how that plays out.

   Sometimes you can't even believe your grandmother.

   That's why you need to have precious stones GIA-certified, and mapped, so you can verify that the stone is authentic and is the one that is promised in the will. When having the stone certified, you have the option of having the stone laser-etched with a microscopic serial number to match the GIA report.

- **Redesign it.** If a piece of jewelry that has sentimental value is sitting in your drawer and you never wear it and no one in your family is likely to want it, remake it into something you will wear. Gerardi told me of a client who was married for many years. After her husband died, she carried her wedding and engagement rings and his wedding ring around for a year in anguish. Gerardi helped her move on. They took pictures of the rings. Then Gerardi removed the diamonds—a total of five—from the rings and had them combined into a single new ring, which the woman wears on her right hand. "No one has to drag around those old rings."

Similarly, I showed Gerardi a large cocktail-style ring my mom used to wear. The gold ring had a swirl of half a dozen dark (not too pretty) sapphires curved around a row of five diamonds. It wasn't my style, but it meant something. I had the diamonds removed and put into a plain white-gold band, which I wear daily. "What you did was perfect," Gerardi said. "You want to preserve the history, not necessarily the ring. Holding on to jewelry in a box serves no one."

- **Recycle the gold.** If it's the gold you hold dear, you can request that a jeweler use the actual gold to make your new piece. Normally, jewelers buy gold in bars that they melt to work with. Taking gold from an existing piece of jewelry requires separating the gold from the alloy it's mixed with to turn it back into its pure state to be reused, which can be done, but it will cost you more.

- **Don't fight about it.** Get the papers in order now, know what you have, and spell out what you want done with it. When fights arise over family jewels, much is lost. As in other areas of legacy litigation, families spend thousands of dollars on lawyers who hire appraisers, only to have the other side hire an appraiser to reappraise it. Regardless of the true value, the meaning is certainly lost forever.

GOOD TO KNOW

Don't overlook pawnshops. For a pair of gold earrings that a jeweler might pay $50 meltdown value for, a pawnshop owner might pay you $150 because he knows he can sell them "as is" quickly. But don't be surprised if you see them in his case the next day for $350. "That's supportable," Gerardi said.

The Tale of the Tainted Diamond

Talking with Christine Gerardi about jewelry, particularly jewelry laden with history, not always positive, made me realize I had a job to do, a diamond to deal with. Not just any diamond, but the one from my former engagement ring, from my former husband.

The diamond was beautiful, over a carat and high quality in color, although its cut, a marquis, was no longer popular. I could have had it made into a pendant or a right-hand ring, but that didn't feel right. I couldn't exactly split it between the girls. So it sat in a drawer.

My feeling has always been that just because that marriage didn't work out doesn't mean it was a mistake. I had these two wonderful children, after all. But the diamond ring, so symbolic, needed to go to someone else.

Fast-forward five years. My daughter Paige and a young man she had known all through high school started dating in college, and eventually became serious. They began talking about marriage. Both were in grad school, living on student budgets. When the subject of a ring came up, I said to Paige in passing, "Well, I have a nice diamond I'm not using." Paige wondered whether she might have it for her ring.

"I don't have a problem with that," I said, "but first we have to ask four other people for permission. We have to ask your dad, your sister, my husband, and your boyfriend whether they mind."

You see how complicated it gets? And we are just talking about a small piece of rock.

Her dad said, "It's fine with me. Your mom will never wear it again." Her sister said, "I don't want it." DC said, "No problem here." And the boyfriend said, "Paige would really like that."

So it was settled. I gave her intended the ring. He had the diamond put in a new setting and proposed. What a lovely way of passing on the family jewels. Paige would have a family diamond, and we could reallocate this family asset. The retail price of a diamond like that would be well out of the young man's student budget, and would also far exceed the amount I could get selling it, such are the markups in the diamond world.

So this was a win-win. Except, the engagement didn't last. The relationship ended. And the diamond ring in its new setting was again in a box in a drawer.

A couple months later, Paige handed me the box. "Here's this back," she said. "This diamond is tainted. Next guy is going to buy me a diamond."

Noted. But now what?

If it hadn't been for my meeting with Gerardi, that diamond would have stayed in the drawer, a victim of my inertia and inexperience in selling jewelry. As a result, down the road, the girls would have one day been saddled with figuring out what to do with this vestige of their parents' broken marriage and Paige's broken engagement.

I wouldn't be leaving an heirloom. I'd be leaving a headache.

I decided to preempt that scenario. I took the diamond in the new setting along with the old setting to a fine jewelry store. There, I had the diamond removed from the new setting. I returned that setting less the center stone to the former fiancé. The jeweler, a graduate gemologist, weighed, measured, and graded the diamond, and told me what his store would buy it for. He would also buy the old setting for melt value.

Before I went that route, however, I did as Gerardi advised and took the stone and the original setting to a pawnshop. Full disclosure, I had never set foot in a pawnshop in my life, so I felt a little out of place. The owner of this particular pawnshop had a good reputation and came highly recommended by both Gerardi and the jeweler-gemologist I'd met with.

Because I would never suggest you do something I hadn't tried myself, I ventured in.

The pawnshop would match, not better the jeweler's offer. I told the jeweler the pawnshop matched his price (no sense bluffing, as all these people talk) and asked if he would raise his offer $100. He did. So I sold the diamond and original setting to the jeweler for exactly one-fourth of what the ring cost new over thirty years ago.

And that was OK. I remembered the words of Tim Luke: "Take the offer." And the tip from the other appraiser, "Would you buy the ring for that?" No. So I took the money and put it in the trust, where it will grow and someday get divided between my girls, which is exactly how this asset should convey. As we said earlier, it's easier to divide cash than a ring.

Was this a hassle? Yes. Would it have been easier to keep the ring in my drawer? Yes. But then my kids would have been stuck dealing with this tainted diamond, and the associated memories, and why have that cloud hovering ahead? I saved them the trouble and that alone was worth if not the money, certainly the effort.

How to Live Forever

Legacy. What is a legacy?
It's planting seeds in a garden you never get to see.

—LIN-MANUEL MIRANDA, American playwright
and composer (1980–)

Throughout this book I have focused a lot on the "how." How to get your papers in order. How to set up an estate. How others have left meaningful legacies. And how to liquidate your belongings so you don't burden your loved ones, and so you can turn material assets into money into meaning. Although getting your papers in order and dealing with your material assets (your tainted diamonds) are laudable, important goals, something else is more important.

The "why."

We are gone from this world for far longer than we're here, so why not aspire to, as Maya Angelou said, "make a mark on the world that can't be erased."

When we look into the night sky, we see light that stars generated millions of years ago. Some of the stars we see tonight may have burned out long ago. Imagine your legacy as a light shining long after you're gone. When designing your legacy, consider the impact the choices you make today could have on others and on the world for generations.

As you've seen throughout this book, you don't need to be rich to make a lasting difference. We've met many people here of minimal means and big hearts. The schoolteacher who left her modest house to benefit generations of students to come is just one example of someone who understood the why.

We saw the why in the gifts thoughtful estate planners left their communities, alma maters, and places of worship, gifts that will provide disadvantaged students with scholarships, animals with homes, rural areas with clean drinking water, gifts that will beautify city gardens, enhance the arts, benefit children with special needs. Gifts that will make the world richer, better.

Of course, I'm not suggesting that we bypass our children, extended families, or loved ones. By all means, take care of them first. But then let a bit spill over to help the world long after you leave it, to keep shining your light far into the future. That extra doesn't have to be much. Just 5 to 10 percent of your estate can go a long way.

And one more thing. As you design your legacy, tell your children, grandchildren, extended family, nieces, nephews, and other loved ones about the why. When the why becomes part of your story, you hand down another, less tangible but possibly more meaningful, benefit.

Your legacy will be measured not by its size, but by its influence. By setting an example for the next generation, they will learn from you, and their children will learn, and their children, and on downstream, how to leave this Earth, and so you create a pattern that simply becomes "what our family does." And your legacy becomes making better people who make a better world into infinity. And that is well enough.

APPENDIX

What to bring to your first meeting with a financial adviser

Asset listing (see asset worksheet in this appendix) and statements related to those assets such as:

Investment Accounts

- ○ Brokerage Accounts
- ○ Mutual Fund Statements
- ○ Annuity Statements
- ○ Children's Assets, Such as 529 Plans or Custodial Accounts
- ○ Investments in Closely Held Businesses

Real Estate

- ○ Personal Residence
- ○ Investment Real Estate
- ○ Retirement Accounts
- ○ 401(k) or 403(b) Accounts
- ○ Pension Statements
- ○ Profit-Sharing Plans
- ○ IRAs

Listing of your liabilities along with term, interest rate, and expected payoff:

- ○ Mortgage
- ○ Home Equity Line
- ○ Business Debt
- ○ Student Loans
- ○ Sources of Income/Expenses/Cash Flow
- ○ Pay Stub
- ○ Expected Bonus
- ○ Business Income

What to bring to your first meeting with a financial adviser *(continued)*

- Flows from Rental Real Estate
- Gifts/Expected Inheritances
- Expected Annual or Monthly Expenditures
- Charitable Giving
- One-Time Large Cash Outflows Such as
  - Real Property Purchase
  - Boat/RV Purchase
  - Vacation Costs

Tax Documents
- Latest Individual Income Tax Return (Form 1040)
- Statement of Capital Gains and Losses for the Current Year
- Summary of Income Tax Basis for Investment Assets
- Last-Filed Gift Tax Return

Insurance Policies
- Life Insurance
- Disability Policies
- Long-Term-Care Insurance

Legal Documents: If you have these bring them:
- Wills
- Designation of Health-Care Surrogates
- Advance Health-Care Directive
- Durable Power of Attorney
- Trust Agreements
- Prenuptial or Postnuptial Agreements

Source: Resource Consulting Group, Orlando

Trusted Advisers

In case I get hit by a meteor, these are the key people to contact.

For my trust/will documents, please contact:

Lawyer's Name   _____

Company   _____

Phone number   _____

Email address   _____

Mailing address   _____

For access to financial information, please contact:

Accountant's Name   _____

Company   _____

Phone number   _____

Email address   _____

Mailing address   _____

For my funeral arrangements, please work with:

Name   _____

Company   _____

Phone number   _____

Email address   _____

Mailing address   _____

What do I have?

What do I own? (Assets)

What do I owe? (Liabilities)

Cash		Debts	
Savings Accounts	$ _____	Credit Card Balances	$ _____
Checking Accounts	_____	Outstanding Bills	_____
Cash on Hand	_____	Income Taxes Owed	_____
Rent Receivables	_____	Property Taxes Owed	_____
Loan Receivables	_____	Alimony	_____
Other	_____	Child Support	_____
TOTAL	_____	TOTAL	_____

Property		Mortgages/Rents	
Value of Residence	$ _____	Residence	$ _____
Second Home Value	_____	Second Home	_____
Income Property	_____	Income Property	_____
Land	_____	Land	_____
Other Properties	_____	Other Properties	_____
TOTAL	_____	TOTAL	_____

Investments		Loans	
Retirement Plans	$ _____	Home Equity	$ _____
Certificates of Deposit	_____	Student	_____
Stocks/Bonds	_____	Bank	_____
Pension Plans	_____	Personal	_____
Mutual Funds	_____	Against Retirement Account	_____
Other	_____	Finance Company	_____
TOTAL	_____	Other Obligations	_____
		TOTAL	_____

continued ▶

What do I have? [continued]

What do I own? (Assets)

Personal Property (Current Cash Value)

Vehicles $ _____

Furnishings   _____

Collectibles   _____

Antiques   _____

Jewelry   _____

Boat/RV   _____

Other   _____

TOTAL   _____

TOTAL ASSETS $ _____

– TOTAL LIABILITIES $ _____

= NET WORTH $ _____

Asset Inventory

To help your estate planner, personal representatives, and beneficiaries recover your assets (in case you get hit by a meteor), use this form to give them the information they will need.

Banking and Investment Accounts

Checking Account

Where Located: _____

Account Number: _____

Who Has Access: _____

Who Is the Named Beneficiary: _____

Savings Account

Where Located: _____

Account Number: _____

Who Has Access: _____

Who Is the Named Beneficiary: _____

Retirement Account

Where Located: _____

Account Number: _____

Who Has Access: _____

Who Is the Named Beneficiary: _____

continued ▶

Asset Inventory (continued)

Certificates of Deposit

Where Located: _____

Account Number: _____

Who Has Access: _____

Who Is the Named Beneficiary: _____

Stocks/Bonds

Where Located: _____

Account Number: _____

Who Has Access: _____

Who Is the Named Beneficiary: _____

Pension Plans

Where Located: _____

Account Number: _____

Who Has Access: _____

Who Is the Named Beneficiary: _____

Asset Inventory (continued)

Mutual Funds

Where Located: _____

Account Number: _____

Who Has Access: _____

Who Is the Named Beneficiary: _____

Safe-Deposit Box

Where Located: _____

Where the Key Is: _____

Who Has Access: _____

Contents: _____

Storage Facility

Where Located: _____

How to Access: _____

Who Has Access: _____

Contents: _____

Household Bills

In case I get struck by a meteor, these are the ongoing household bills that will need to be addressed either by paying off the amounts or terminating the service. (Please note any payments that get automatically deducted from my bank account.)

House Mortgage or Rent Payment

Lender/Landlord:

Account Number: _____

Monthly Amount: _____

Car Payment

Lender: _____

Account Number: _____

Monthly Amount: _____

Credit Card(s), Including Department Stores

Company: _____

Account Number: _____

Company: _____

Account Number: _____

Company: _____

Account Number: _____

Household Bills *(continued)*

Utilities (Gas, Electric, Water, Landline):

Company Name: _____

Account Number: _____

Company Name: _____

Account Number: _____

Company Name: _____

Account Number: _____

Company Name: _____

Account Number: _____

Cell phone

Company Name: _____

Account Number: _____

Cable/Internet Service

Company Name: _____

Account Number: _____

continued ▶

Household Bills (continued)

Car Insurance

Company Name: _____

Account Number: _____

Payment Amount/Frequency _____

Property Insurance

Company Name: _____

Account Number: _____

Payment Amount/Frequency _____

Medical Insurance

Company Name: _____

Account Number: _____

Payment Amount/Frequency _____

Gardening Service

Company Name: _____

Account Number: _____

Payment Amount/Frequency _____

Household Bills (continued)

Pest Control

Company Name: _____

Account Number: _____

Payment Amount/Frequency _____

Security Service

Company Name: _____

Account Number: _____

Payment Amount/Frequency _____

Other Recurring Bills

_____

_____

_____

_____

_____

_____

Attached to this worksheet is a list of all digital accounts, such as social media (Facebook, LinkedIn, Instagram), entertainment (Netflix, Hulu, Pandora), and shopping accounts (Amazon Prime) that will need to be closed. Include user names and passwords.

What matters?

Who matters to me? (These could be children, partners, parents, siblings, grandchildren, friends, pets.)

_____

_____

_____

_____

_____

_____

_____

What places have been important in my life and have helped form who I am today? (Your hometown or community, your schools, your church or synagogue, a place you may have frequently visited over the course of your life and connect with.)

_____

_____

_____

_____

_____

_____

_____

_____

What matters? *(continued)*

How do I find joy? (Hiking, painting, worshipping, learning, listening to music, helping others.)

_____

_____

_____

_____

_____

What has been the focus of my life's work?

_____

_____

_____

_____

_____

Beyond the necessities, what do I spend my money on?

_____

_____

_____

_____

_____

continued ▶

What matters? *(continued)*

What problems in this world do I believe need fixing? (Homelessness, drug abuse, teen suicide, racial tension, gender inequality, domestic violence, a specific medical disease or mental health condition, pollution, animal cruelty, etc.)

_____

_____

_____

_____

_____

_____

_____

_____

What am I grateful for? (My education, my book club, my hometown.)

_____

_____

_____

_____

_____

_____

What matters? (continued)

What charities have I supported in the past, and of those, which ones would I like to continue to support? Similarly, given what I cherish, what other charities or types of charities might be a good fit for my contributions?

_____

_____

_____

_____

_____

_____

_____

_____

_____

_____

ACKNOWLEDGMENTS

When first asked to write a book on legacy, and, well, everything that goes into that, I felt both honored and daunted. Few topics seem more important, after all. Fortunately, I had behind me what anyone needs to accomplish a tall task—someone who believes that you can do it and that you are the one to do it.

For having the idea for this book, for singling me out as the one to write it, and for his faith in me, I thank Matthew Lore, my extraordinary editor, who deserves at least as much credit, and probably more, for this book being here as I do. For her encouragement, wisdom and advice, I thank my stellar agent Linda Konner.

Even still, writing a book like this can at times feel like swimming across the English Channel entangled with an octopus. Fortunately, what got me to the other side is what always gets me through—leaning on others.

For fielding my questions and for sharing their significant professional expertise, I am immensely grateful to Kurt Aumann, Amy Davis, Brian Fogle, Emily Blaugrund Fox, Barry Gordon, Duncan McLean, Anthony Palma, Tommy Thomas, Mark Yegsigian, Howard Zaritsky, and Carol Zurcher.

For trusting me with their personal stories, I am indebted to Arlene Cogen, Tom Finnie, Virginia and Ed Fulz, Gloria Galanes, Cindy Lopez, Caroline Marshall, "Charlie Quinn," Deborah Robison, and Kim Trent. I sincerely appreciate the financial experts who read behind me, including my dear friend Tracy Ramos, and Barbara Yeager.

For their editorial chops, and for making me look better than I am, I am indebted to the meticulous team at The Experiment: Nancy Elgin, Zach Pace, Hannah Matuszak, and, for the book's cover art, Beth Bugler.

Last but far from least, I am grateful beyond measure to my husband and personal in-house counsel, Doug Carey, who, as I embarked on the task of writing a book about leaving your legacy, and all the legalities that go with that, ordered the latest law casebook on estates and trusts, read the entire 1,027-page tome, and boiled it down for me, so I could boil it down further for you. Doug not only read and distilled into a nutshell a lot of complicated material, but also fielded my many legal questions, rolling back the fog until this once foreign world made sense to me, and I hope, now to you.

As Matthew often and so appreciatively said, *thanks all around*.

INDEX

ABOUT THE AUTHOR

MARNI JAMESON is America's most beloved home-and-lifestyle columnist. Besides writing a weekly nationally syndicated column, Jameson is the author of five bestselling books, including her Downsizing the Family Home series. "At Home with Marni Jameson," Marni's popular syndicated column, appears weekly in more than twenty papers nationwide, reaching five million readers with her trademark humor and advice. The mother of a blended family of five grown children, Marni lives in Winter Park, Florida, with her husband, Doug, and their three unruly dogs.

marnijameson.com | 🅵 At Home with Marni Jameson | 🅣 marniathome